"*Marriage on the Men...* ... First Baptist in marriage c... ...leship course. The Braggs u... ...ouples build, or rebuild, the ... .on. By understanding the role of prayer, maneuvering through road blocks, avoiding pitfalls, dealing with ruins of the past, and guarding the gates, I have witnessed many couples find hope for the future. Clint and Penny have lived these truths in their own marriage and graciously share these great tools for others to use. In a day of marriage confusion, this is a timely message firmly rooted in God's truth."

Dr. Mel Blackaby, Author and senior pastor of
First Baptist Church, Jonesboro, Georgia

"We encourage couples to read this book, no matter where they are in their marriage. Clint and Penny Bragg are trusted marriage champions, having served couples in our church and trained marriage ministry leaders in our community. We are confident that God will use this book to strengthen marriages and families."

Bubba and Cindy Cathy, Owners of WinShape, Rome, Georgia

"From marriage enrichment to marriage crisis, *Marriage on the Mend* has the tools all couples need! Practical, easy tools that any couple can implement right away to make a difference in their relationship."

Eric and Jennifer Garcia, Cofounders of the Association of
Marriage and Family Ministries

"*Marriage on the Mend* is a unique and long-overdue book for any couple who wants to strengthen their relationship and put it on the road to healing, peace, and joy. Penny and Clint Bragg know the truth of every word in this book because they've lived it. They know the hopelessness of a marriage lost—and they know the delight of a marriage restored. And the beautiful part is that out of their experience comes a passion to now help other couples realize and uncover the extraordinary potential in their marriages. The Braggs are the real deal. And this book should be required reading for any couple who wants not only a restored but a *thriving* marriage."

Ginger Kolbaba, author of *Surprised by Remarriage* and former editor of *Marriage Partnership* magazine

"Clint and Penny are part of an amazing story of God's commitment, grace, and redemptive glory. They are devoted servants of Christ and marriage missionaries. Their story will inspire and encourage you, and grow your faith in a God who is for marriage and never gives up!"

Robert S. Paul, Vice president of Focus on the Family's National Institute of Marriage

"Marriage is a wonderful, miraculous, supernatural gift from God. It is at the heart of family, and the family advances God's kingdom in the world, generation upon generation. Because of this, Satan and the demons launch some of their fiercest attacks against husbands and wives! Is your marriage in trouble? You don't need a few tools and tips for better communication; you need a miracle from God to change your hearts and transform your relationship. The Scriptures that Clint and Penny share in this book have the power to make that miracle a reality!"

Dr. Rob Rienow, Founder of Visionary Family Ministries

"At last! Here is a book for couples who want to put their marriage back together and find healing but don't know how to do it. Chapter by chapter, *Marriage on the Mend* walks a couple through the process of reconciliation so they are able to pick up the pieces of a broken marriage and build a strong and joy-filled relationship. Clint and Penny Bragg know what it takes to get past the roadblocks, triumph over traumatic triggers, rebuild trust, and find forgiveness. They use their own amazing story of restoration and the stories of others, as well as scriptural insights and practical strategies to help couples finally achieve the marriage they've always wanted."

Linda W. Rooks, Author of *Broken Heart on Hold: Surviving Separation*

"I have known and coached many marriages needing a blueprint to mend. And I know Clint and Penny Bragg. The book you are holding is a solid, biblical blueprint for bringing hope, restoration, and biblical truth to your marriage. Chapter 6 alone, 'Rebuilding on the Ruins of Your Past,' is worth the price of the book. Read it, pass copies on to others, and hold onto your copy as part of your legacy of restoration and gratitude!"

Dr. Gary and Barb Rosberg, Authors of
6 Secrets to a Lasting Love and cofounders
of America's Family Coaches

"Clint and Penny Bragg are truly marriage missionaries. Their book, *Marriage on the Mend*, focuses on tools that help every marriage. God gives us marriage as a chance to love, know, and follow Him with all of our heart, mind, soul, and strength. This book helps us do that!"

Jeff and Cheryl Scruggs, Authors of *I Do Again*, and
their family's book, *Still LoLo*, and cofounders of
Hope Matters Marriage Ministries

"There are many marriage books written by wise and gifted professionals. But what Dave Ramsey says about finances we believe is also true about marriage: 'It's twenty percent knowledge and eighty percent behavior.' That behavior and how to achieve it is what Clint and Penny Bragg offer in this book. Real life. Real practices. Real emotions. The reality of what happens behind closed doors aligning with God's plan and purpose for marriage. We work with couples in the midst of adultery recovery. Clint and Penny offer them the next steps to keeping the marriage they've saved healthy. Although their testimony alone blesses many, we believe what they've learned and shared within these pages will bless innumerably more."

Gary and Mona Shriver, Authors of *Unfaithful: Hope &
Healing After Infidelity* and cofounders of
Hope & Healing Ministries, Inc.

"As a couple, Clint and Penny Bragg are uniquely qualified to help any marriage in need of restoration. Just reading their story will inspire faith in your heart that God can fix your marriage. But *Marriage on the Mend* offers so much more than inspiration. It's a wonderfully practical and relevant book filled with insights and specific guidance, enough to help any couple find their way back to that narrow road that leads to life."

Dan Walsh, Award-winning fiction author of ten novels including the best-selling Restoration series coauthored with Dr. Gary Smalley

"We know Clint and Penny and their story. The reconciliation tools they teach are not based on head knowledge. They are based on real-life experiences that were learned during one of the most amazing saved marriage journeys we have ever known. Any couple who is serious about making their marriage work will benefit beyond their wildest expectations when they follow the principles in this book."

Joe and Michelle Williams, Authors of *Yes, Your Marriage Can Be Saved* and cofounders of Marriage 911 God's Way

Marriage
on the Mend

PROPERTY OF
ST BAPTIST CHURCH
GEORGE, IOWA

Marriage
on the Mend

Healing Your Relationship After
Crisis, Separation, or Divorce

CLINT *and* PENNY A. BRAGG

Kregel
Publications

Marriage on the Mend: Healing Your Relationship After Crisis, Separation, or Divorce
© 2015 by Clint and Penny A. Bragg

Published by Kregel Publications, a division of Kregel, Inc., 2450 Oak Industrial Dr. NE, Grand Rapids, MI 49505.

All rights reserved. No part of this book may be reproduced, stored in a retrieval system, or transmitted in any form or by any means—electronic, mechanical, photocopy, recording, or otherwise—without written permission of the publisher, except for brief quotations in reviews.

The authors and publisher are not engaged in rendering medical or psychological services, and this book is not intended as a guide to diagnose or treat medical or psychological problems. If medical, psychological, or other expert assistance is required by the reader, please seek the services of your own health care provider or certified counselor.

The QR codes provided in this book are included to enhance the reader's interaction with the author and the text. Kregel takes no responsibility for the content accessed by the links and cannot guarantee the links will remain active for the life of this book.

Scriptures quotations are from the Holy Bible, New International Version®, NIV®. Copyright © 1973, 1978, 1984, 2011 by Biblica, Inc.™ Used by permission of Zondervan. All rights reserved worldwide. www.zondervan.com

ISBN 978-0-8254-4234-6

Printed in the United States of America
15 16 17 18 19 / 5 4 3 2 1

*To Jesus the mediator of a new covenant,
and to the sprinkled blood that speaks a
better word than the blood of Abel.*

<small>HEBREWS 12:24</small>

Contents

Acknowledgments

Properly acknowledging every person who has had a hand in birthing this book causes us to lavish God with gratitude. Only He could have orchestrated such a feat involving so many gifted people. May we steward well all that He has freely given us through the ministry of reconciliation. All this is from God's gracious hand.

Heartfelt gratitude to our loving families who sacrifice our presence in California so families across the nation and abroad can find healing.

We gratefully acknowledge our monthly supporters who allow us to serve as marriage missionaries through the generosity of their faithful offerings and relentless prayers. You fuel our journey in every way. Richard and Sharon Williams, we bless you and thank you for the substantial investment you have sown into our ministry throughout the years.

Thank you to every courageous couple who allowed us to put their story in this book. Peeling back your marriage and letting the world look inside it is not an easy thing. You are our heroes!

We appreciate all those who dedicated their time and skill to proofreading the manuscript and providing us with helpful feedback: John and Becky Duck, Dan and Pam Fitzgerald, and Connie Pryce. In addition, we acknowledge those who have shown their support for this project from the beginning: Micki Ann Harris, Annie Jones, Joe and Dawn Nassise, Dr. Johnathan and Penny Mun, Dr. Dale Hummel, Kathy Coryell, Mona Shriver, Michelle

Williams, Clifford F. and Doris Asher, Irene Kenna, Ted and Elizabeth Sundburg, Lorenzo Bronzini, and Sue Senadenos. Linda Rooks, we bless you for suggesting the Florida Christian Writers Conference, a turning point in finally getting published.

Thank you to our marriage mentors, Dale and Colleen Goncalves, and our ministry mentors, Joe and Michelle Williams, who keep us on the straight and narrow.

Micki Ann Harris, we blame you for planting the seed for this book in a coffee shop so many years ago by asking, "What about Nehemiah?" and then handing us your treasured study notes.

Eric and Jennifer Garcia, we celebrate you, our Reconciling Troubled Marriages Ministry Team, and the entire AMFM family. You invited us to serve alongside you in ministry and have continually opened door after door for us with profound grace.

Special thanks to Machelle Vallance and WAPN Radio in Holly Hill, Florida, for giving us a voice over the airwaves; and to the Volusia County Word Weavers, who prayed and offered wisdom to help us refine our writing each month.

We offer our deepest gratitude to our Board of Directors: Dale and Colleen Goncalves, Scott and Cathy Jones, and Brian Arvin. You have knelt down alongside Inverse Ministries, Inc. from the very start, offering us godly counsel, encouragement, and prayer.

Amanda Luedeke, our agent extraordinaire, we applaud you. May you and the MacGregor staff be blessed for finding the proper placement for this child. In addition, we're grateful to Steve Barclift, Dawn Anderson, Sarah De Mey, Noelle Pederson, Leah Mastee, and the entire Kregel team for taking a risk on these two rookies. Thank you to our wise and patient editor, Bob Hartig. This is our dream come true.

Introduction

Every broken marriage has the hope of becoming a saved marriage. Why? Because there is *no* relationship in such a state of ruin that it remains beyond God's reach. In our ministry to couples across the nation and abroad, we conclude our testimony by sharing this truth: "If God can reconcile *our* marriage, He can reconcile yours." This is our message to you as well.

There's no way we ever should have reconciled. Pronounced dead in 1991, our marriage was lowered into a grave and buried in the dirt for over a decade. Enter God.

With one mighty breath, He raised our relationship from the dead in 2002, and He's been breathing new life into us ever since.

God can save your marriage too. Perhaps there's so much rubble in your relationship you find that hard to believe. That's okay. Resurrection has a history of being quite unbelievable. But we must ask you to consider this: What if it's true? What if He can?

It is upon this premise that we've written *Marriage on the Mend*. God desires to completely heal every gaping wound in your marriage. What if you allow Him to do the very thing His heart longs for?

One letter, written years ago, started the restoration process in our marriage. It is our earnest prayer that this book will do the same for you.

Chapter 1

Honoring the Process

We are living proof that, against all odds, God can mend a marriage. Originally married to each other on September 2, 1989, we sailed through our first year together without incident. But by our second year of marriage, irritations and differences that were once fairly benign began to create a steady stream of conflict. Our prayers for a permanent solution—or at least a quick fix—remained unanswered. Before long, we couldn't agree on anything, including the source of our discontent. Something was definitely broken, and try as we might, we just couldn't fix it. To complicate matters, we were too proud to tell anyone that our relationship was on the rocks. As a result, the emotional, physical, and spiritual breach between us only widened.

The fragile state of our marriage created the perfect scenario for me (Penny) to start looking elsewhere for comfort. Clint confronted me about his suspicions regarding an affair, but I vehemently denied his accusations. The tension between us mounted, until one balmy evening just prior to our second anniversary, I packed a few things into a suitcase and rolled it out our front door. The last time we saw each other was the day our divorce papers were notarized, citing that "irreconcilable differences have caused the permanent breakdown of our marriage."

Fast forward eleven years, three thousand coast-to-coast miles, and a series of divinely orchestrated events. On August 17, 2002, we were married again in front of our family and friends. Throughout the remainder of this book, we'll share more of our story. What's important for you to know right now is that even though God reconciled our marriage, we incorrectly assumed the hard part was behind us. Shortly after saying "I do" for the second time, we discovered that nothing could be further from the truth.

This is just one of the unique scenarios couples initially face after deciding they want to make their marriage work. Depending on the history of the relationship, other complications also enter in and cloud the mix, such as past betrayal, financial deficits, lack of intimacy, and the unsupportive opinions of others. The emotional pain of such things feels unbearable. Learning to love the same person anew is daunting, and attempts to toss in the towel can unexpectedly resurface. We know this place of despair, and if any of what we've described sounds like your situation, we know the intensity of your pain.

Marriage is messy, and reconciling a relationship after a crisis, separation, divorce, or all of the above is even messier. You will face problems, old and new, along the way. But you are not alone. We had our fair share of troubles too, just like every other couple we've met. People often tell us that the problems contributing to the fragmentation of their marriages are far too ugly for repairs *ever* to be made. They aren't ready to get real with God or each other; therefore, they seriously doubt their relationship can be mended. That is a lie. If you sincerely want to get well and you want your marriage to get well, then you're already on the road to wholeness and healing.

Depending upon your marriage history, the rebuilding process may seem complicated right now. That's normal. Make no mistake: the restoration of a marriage is both incredibly euphoric and agonizingly painful. Expect the process to take time and hard work. Unfortunately, it's much easier to fight than to forgive.

There were many times when we honestly disclosed our mistakes before God and each other and wept over the consequences of our sins and shortcomings. During those times, we wanted nothing more than to cover our heads, tuck our respective tails between our legs, and part ways again in sulking defeat. However, engaging in the hard work of reestablishing our marriage covenant has yielded rewards beyond anything we ever thought possible. The shedding of Christ's blood—combined with our own sweat and tears—has resulted in wholeness and healing that is incomparable in worth or measure.

The same can be said of your marriage. Your restoration begins with your answering yes to the two questions we ask all the couples who contact us for help: Are you at the bottom of the bottom? And, do you want to get well?

Would Our Marriage Make It?

According to a study conducted by the Barna Group, "Among those who have said their wedding vows, one out of three have been divorced at least once."[1] National divorce rates are said to be on the rise, but statistics are sketchy at best regarding the percentage of couples who successfully reconcile after a crisis or separation, or who remarry their former spouse after a divorce. It's safe to assume that couples who reconcile definitely do not have the odds stacked in their favor. Neither did we.

"Our marriage has to make it this time!" I (Penny) cried as we stood arguing in the kitchen shortly after remarrying each other. Our honeymoon high had lasted about as long as our wedding day. Once the reception was over and the guests had gone, we hit conflict. The source of our disagreement paled next to the stark realization that our marriage would fail again if we didn't get some help. We loved each other and God, but our first marriage had proved those things alone simply weren't enough.

"Are you going to leave me again?" Clint asked with tears rolling down his cheeks. The honesty and vulnerability of his question bowled me over backward. Of course I wasn't going to leave him again, but that first disagreement after remarrying triggered some painful memories of previous conflicts, and neither of us knew what to do about it. It took days to sort through the clutter, expose our true feelings, and acknowledge our fears.

"There has to be another way to do this," I sobbed as we sat down to sort things out several nights later. As Clint and I discussed what had led up to our disagreement, we realized that God had captured our full attention during the standoff. The source of our conflict centered on something rather trivial, but it wasn't the magnitude of it that mattered. The real problem was that we had no proactive plan to resolve conflict—large or small—inevitable in every normal marriage. What made matters even more challenging was that our marriage was far from any norm we'd ever known.

We'd never heard of anyone whose marriage was successfully mended after spending as many years apart as we had. In vain, we began to search for resources that specifically spoke to the unique challenges of restoring a broken marriage. That desperate search is what, years down the road, has led us to write this book. It is the culmination of everything we learned about restoring our relationship during the first five years of our remarriage. Every tool we share is one we faithfully practice in our own marriage to this day, and each one is designed to help you navigate the troubled waters that accompany your decision to reconcile.

True Restoration Takes Time

In our current work as full-time marriage missionaries, we travel across the nation on 40-Day Marriage Mission Trips, sharing our testimony of reconciliation and assisting couples who have lost all hope of healing. Not only have we experienced the full restoration of our own relationship, but we've also witnessed countless other couples who have overcome the odds.

Our own testimony is quite extraordinary. In this chapter, we share a small portion of it with you to emphasize this important fact: true restoration takes time, and you must honor your unique process. Eleven years may seem a bit extreme, but our story illustrates that God's processes and timelines are as important, if not more important, than the final outcome. During our years apart, major overhauls had to happen in our individual hearts. After we finally remarried, we had yet another long road ahead.

Once a couple decides they want to work things out, there is a sense of urgency to immediately "fix" all the problems from the past. However, you must be willing to respect *whatever* timelines God uses to heal your relationship and to entrust the entire process to Him.

Consider this: it probably took a while for your marriage to get to the point of crisis, separation, and/or divorce. Troubles in a marriage rarely surface overnight; your difficult circumstances and conflicts have most likely mounted over time. It will likewise take time for your relationship to heal. But no matter what your situation is today, if you accept that it will take ample time to get the relationship properly realigned and back onto the road, you can make significant progress at an early stage.

Perhaps you have experienced such repeated discord that you separated. Some of you may have even gone as far as divorce, like we did. There is hope! Even the darkest detours of your relationship (i.e., infidelity, addiction, abuse, bankruptcy, etc.) can be completely transformed when you're both willing to submit your hearts to God. If you truly want to get well, God will do His part as you do yours.

However, before we continue, let us clarify an important point: While every marriage can be saved, there are extenuating circumstances that must be acknowledged when safety is a concern. If you, your children, or any member of your family is in physical danger as a result of your spouse's behavior, get law enforcement and other necessary professionals involved immediately. Your safety and that of your loved ones supersedes everything else.

Once we realized it was going to take time for us to restore our own relationship, we made a very important agreement that we'd like you to consider for yourselves. It was this: during our first year back together, we consciously made the restoration of our marriage our top priority, second only to our individual relationships with God. We wanted God to know we were serious about devoting quality time to healing our marriage. We hadn't been intentional about our relationship the first time around; this time we would be.

Because we both tended to overcommit our schedules, our agreement ensured that we weren't running ahead of God. We agreed not to take on new responsibilities or endeavors during that first year of remarriage and restoration. Promotions, projects, or leadership opportunities, no matter how exciting or noble, were turned down or put on hold. Our agreement also included not accepting offers to serve in any ongoing roles at our church. If that seems selfish, consider: we knew that if we didn't get intentional about mending our marriage, we would be of no service to God or our church.

Instead of balancing a bunch of new responsibilities, we attended church, worshipped God side by side, listened attentively to our pastor's sermons, and talked to couples we could trust. We attended marriage conferences and workshops we knew would benefit us. We also committed to reading and discussing several Christian books together. This intentionality had a profound impact on our restoration. In hindsight, we could have helped our cause more by explaining our priorities to our pastors, family members, close friends, and colleagues. Then they would have understood the importance we were placing on our marriage this time around. Please learn from our mistake and communicate the emphasis you're placing on your marriage to the people who are close to you. Doing so will strengthen your support system and alleviate misunderstandings about the choices you make.

During the coming months, you'll need guidance as you reassess, regroup, and prayerfully rebuild your relationship. There are many ideas in this book that will help you gain and maintain perspective. Although the drama of marital conflict may differ drastically from one couple to the next, the time and tools it takes to mend marriages are very similar.

Woven throughout this text is sound advice from couples who have done (and continue to do) the hard work of restoring their marriages, as well as helpful bits and pieces from our own experiences. While each couple featured is unique, all have several things in common. Most importantly, they know that God saved their marriage. Also, they came out on the other side of their crisis far more spiritually and relationally wealthy than when they entered it.

While these couples share similarities, every marriage survival story is unique, depending upon the nature of the crisis (or crises) that contributed to its breakdown. The ways in which God restores one relationship may not be exactly the same ways He restores another.

Learning from the Past

None of the examples in this book should take precedence over the truths in God's Word. In light of that, written accounts from the experiences of Nehemiah are threaded throughout almost every chapter. Although Nehemiah's task of rebuilding the war-torn walls of Jerusalem clearly was not recorded with troubled marriages in mind, it is a perfect biblical parallel for restoring your relationship.

At the opening of Nehemiah, a representative remnant of the Israelite nation had just returned to Jerusalem after seventy years of Babylonian exile. God sent them prophets and leaders to restore their community, which included rebuilding the massive wall surrounding the city. Enter Nehemiah. Against fierce opposition, social and economic devastation, threats of attack, chronic sin, and evildoers who repeatedly attempted to stop him, this persevering leader succeeded in completing what God called him to accomplish. You'll discover principles in Nehemiah that, like the Jewish people rebuilding their city, can help you rebuild your relationship.

There is no set pace for proceeding through this book and the tools we share. Remember, true healing in all broken relationships takes time. So resist the temptation to skip over implementing the tools or rushing through the pages. At the end of each chapter, you will find a prayer to help facilitate your healing.

Be sure to complete the exercises and discussion questions at the end of each chapter. Also, use your smartphone to scan the QR codes embedded within the text. These codes will link you to our free video podcasts that expand upon the tools in this book. If you don't have a QR code reader, you can access the videos via inverseministries .org. These videos and extensions are designed to help your relationship become more resilient. Repeat any of these exercises and watch the videos again as time passes and your relationship changes. Trust this book's advice the way you would a wise mentor. We'd like nothing more than to walk beside you through each page. It is a humble privilege to use our past to help change your future.

Before you continue to read any further, take time to pray. Ask God to help you get the most from what we've written. Ask Him to help you learn from your past as well as from ours and the other couples in this book. Let Him know you're willing to be participants in this process. Acknowledge that He is in total control of both your ruins and your restoration. What's happening in your marriage right now is far greater than just the two of you. Your children, extended family, and friends are significantly affected as well. Never minimize the magnitude of what you are about to begin. Restoring your relationship will undoubtedly impact the current generation as well as generations to come. The reconciliation of one marriage under God possesses the power to change families and even nations throughout the world, alter the course of human history, and ultimately, increase the population of heaven. That's what matters most.

In order to effectively maneuver around the roadblocks you'll encounter together, make a conscious and irrevocable decision to choose reconciliation each day for the rest of your lives, especially amid the trials and turbulence that occur as a natural part of mending your marriage. In the next chapter, we'll help you recognize specific roadblocks that may be threatening to impede your progress before you even get started.

Introduction to the Series · *4:29 minutes*

Prayer for the Process of Restoration

Teach us, Father, to place all our demands and desires for the restoration of this relationship in Your hands. Transform them into the desire to be strong and steadfast in You. When we are weak, You are strong and You receive the glory. Be the Lord of what's left of our time together. We relinquish all of our hours and expectations for this marriage to You. Help us not to hoard time in order to serve our private agendas. We cannot condemn anyone, including ourselves, for the time we've lost, and we let go of the time yet before us. We place You in charge of our ruins and their restoration. And we let go of hurriedness in order to truly experience Your healing. We want to get well, God. Heal us. In Jesus' name. Amen.

For a Marriage on the Mend

Make a Timeline

Create a timeline of your marriage that spans the last five years. If you haven't been married very long, modify the timeline to fit your needs. (Option: you may want to start your timeline on your wedding day and work forward from there. The choice is yours.)

Begin by drawing a horizontal line across a large piece of butcher paper. Above the line, list the major physical, emotional, financial, logistical, and spiritual life events that have *positively* impacted your relationship. Below the line, list the major physical, emotional, financial, logistical, and spiritual life events that have *negatively* impacted your relationship.

It's normal for spouses to differ regarding what each one considers a positive or negative life event. As a result, the same event may be listed in both the upper and lower sections of the timeline. For example, a husband feels his job promotion was a positive life event, while his wife feels it was negative because he was often away on business and she was left to care for the children.

Completing this project will take more than one sitting as you think about all of the life events in your marriage history. As you remember more details, add them to the timeline. This timeline will serve as an insightful way to trace some of your current conflicts back to their original sources. See the sample to help get you started.

Questions to Consider

1. What did you notice about your relationship after reviewing the major life events on the timeline?
2. While creating the timeline, were you in agreement about which things you viewed as positive and negative? Why or why not?

3. What else did you notice as you looked back over the events/
   years?
4. Can you see how events or changes might have led up to a crisis
   in your relationship?
5. Read Nehemiah 1–2. What did you notice about his approach
   to rebuilding the wall of Jerusalem? How did Nehemiah set
   out to deal with the restoration process, and how does this
   relate to your marriage?

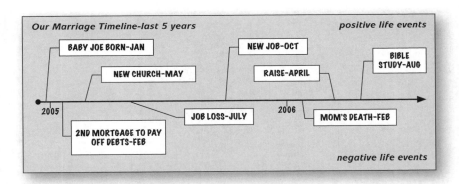

Chapter 2

Recognizing Your Roadblocks

Imagine you have decided to venture out together for a long drive. You've taken the day off work, packed the car, and precisely mapped out your adventure. Everything runs smoothly at first. Then after driving for several hours, you come to an unexpected roadblock and are forced to stop the car. At this point you face an important decision, and there are several options to consider.

You could heed the sign, turn the car around, and find another way to get to your destination. Or you might choose to go someplace else. Another possibility might be to turn off the engine, wait for another car to approach the roadblock, follow their lead, and see how it all turns out for them. Perhaps you would take a more risky approach: ignore the roadblock, move it out of the way, and continue down the road, regardless of the consequences.

Your decision regarding this roadblock hinges on many contributing factors. Is there really something dangerous up ahead? If so, how dangerous is it? Are you afraid? Was the roadblock erected to protect you? Or was it put there as a detour? Are past experiences, emotions, or other issues contributing to your decision? Have you ever faced this roadblock before? If so, what did you do and what was the outcome? What does your spouse think you should do? Do you agree with him or her? What impact is this one choice going to have on your plans? On your marriage? On your children?

We use this example to demonstrate what often occurs when couples reconcile and come face-to-face with their first challenge. It's not just the roadblock that must be considered. Depending upon a couple's history, there can be many other things that factor into the scenario and complicate matters. All of this can become quite overwhelming.

Many of the apparent roadblocks you'll face as you restore your relationship represent opportunities God places in your path to teach you, correct you, and reveal His vision for your marriage. Some of your roadblocks may occur as a result of the consequences of sins or problems from the past. Others are part of a greater spiritual battle. The Enemy wants you to look for a way out of your relationship. He hates a strong marriage. The only way to know what you should do about a roadblock in your relationship is to expose its nature, find out who erected it, surrender it to God, and ask Him to help you understand the reason(s) it was put there.

The Road of Restoration

Reread the subtitle above. Note that it says, "The Road *of* Restoration," not, "The Road *to* Restoration." There's a big difference between the two. The ongoing nature of restoration is a lifestyle and a choice, not simply a destination at which your marriage will arrive. As with any journey, there will be obstacles, some natural and some supernatural. You must learn to discern between the two.

Due to the nature of our divorce and the eleven-year gap that had elapsed before we reconciled, we faced some overwhelming obstacles and needed help. As is often the case with couples who reunite, it seemed as if there was roadblock after roadblock in almost every area of our new life together. In desperation, several nights after our first disagreement, we sat down at the kitchen table to make a list of all our roadblocks. Our list included financial burdens, communication problems, family matters, and more. As far as I (Clint) was concerned, these were huge obstacles in our relationship. In hindsight, I realize that although we thought we'd compiled a pretty complete list that night, it couldn't include the things only God could see coming down the road. It's probably a good thing we didn't know what was about to hit us.

During the first few months of our remarriage, it seemed that every time we turned a corner and made a little headway, we faced yet another challenge. For example, in order to make it to California in time for our wedding, I'd driven over three thousand miles in three days. As a result, I was exhausted. Once I got there, I had to unload my things at Penny's house and then go meet the couple who was going to take me in during the days before our wedding. Most of my belongings remained in boxes for weeks, and I felt disorganized because I didn't have time to unpack before starting my new job. While I was grateful for a teaching position in the district where Penny was employed, I was still considered a new teacher. Therefore the district required me to attend special training that started just two days after our wedding. There was no time to be alone with Penny or get away for a honeymoon.

Penny's assignment as an elementary school principal demanded all of her energy, and she was used to giving it the time it required. Now she had a husband to consider. Although she wouldn't admit it, she was struggling to strike a balance. In addition to these circumstances, rumors surfaced in our district about the "real reasons" behind our divorce. The stress began building inside both of us.

Finances were another major concern. Penny and I had been apart for such a long time that we didn't realize how awkward it would feel to merge our savings, retirement accounts, and other investments, as well as take on each other's debts. To complicate matters,

I still had some burdens from investments that had gone sour while I was living in Florida. It also took six months for my house there to finally sell, so we had two mortgage payments. The resulting stress became so intense for me that, after stuffing it all down inside for several months, I passed out on the locker-room floor one day, and school officials had to call an ambulance. By the time they rushed me to the hospital, massive welts had covered my body like continents on a world map. After running some tests, the doctors were able to determine that I had experienced a rare form of anaphylactic shock. Stress had taken its toll.

Would Our History Repeat Itself?

I (Penny) wanted so much for our marriage to make it this time. After all, I was the one who walked out on Clint so many years ago. For the first few weeks, I was still in a state of shock about our remarriage. Each morning, I woke up and reached my hand across the bed to make sure Clint was really there. While I was grateful for all that had happened, I also began to experience the self-imposed pressure of wanting to be a better wife this time around. Honestly, I wasn't even sure what a better wife should look like.

In addition to these feelings and my concern over what happened to Clint in the locker room, there were relationships within both of our families that still needed to be healed. Not only had I walked out on Clint years ago, but I'd turned my back on his family as well. Our reconciliation called for some awkward face-to-face conversations. I felt so uncomfortable at our first holiday get-together, knowing that everyone in Clint's extended family knew the unpleasant details of our divorce. They were gracious, but I couldn't help feeling like all eyes were on me.

The night we compiled our roadblocks at the kitchen table, we took turns giving input and adding obstacles to the list. Nothing was too small to be overlooked or invalidated. We included challenges such as handling our different styles of communication, clearing financial debts, finding a new home church, reconciling relationships in our families, and developing the marital values we had missed the first time around. Even though neither of us had remarried during our eleven years apart, we still had to deal with the consequences of relationships we'd been involved in during that time. Those issues were also added.

Clint and Penny's Roadblocks

- Selling Clint's home in Florida
- Finding a home to call our own
- Growing friendships with other couples
- Finding a church home we both agree on
- Making connections for Clint in California
- Dealing with past relationships/issues
- Balancing our marriage with work
- Working through communication styles/differences
- Resolving major financial debt
- Finishing Clint's schooling

Once we listed our roadblocks, we surrendered each one to God in prayer. While the odds of our making it past them seemed slim to none at best, we somehow sensed God's promise to use these roadblocks for purposes we could not yet see. Regardless of how bleak things appeared, after that night we were filled with renewed faith that God would send help. Rather than being paralyzed by our problems, we committed to focusing on God's promises regarding them.

As the Holy Spirit stirred our hearts, God showed us how to progressively chip away at all the things that obstructed our path.

Months passed, and we kept track of His answers to our prayers on that same piece of paper.

By the end of our first year back together, we noticed significant progress with each roadblock. More importantly, we were stunned to see that God had taken every obstacle and used it to show us how to walk through those challenges united as *one flesh*.

As a testimony of God's faithfulness, the power of prayer, and the importance of strengthening our individual relationships with Him, we saved that piece of paper. To this day we reflect on the ways God responded, especially when we need to remember what He'll do when we're humble, intentional, prayerful, willing, obedient, and united. In our seminars for couples, we pull out that list to show them the hard evidence of what God did when we finally took responsibility for our own actions, gave Him full permission to change our hearts, and allowed Him to shape our marriage. God longs to do the same for you as well.

Nehemiah's Roadblocks

Before the work on Jerusalem's wall ever got started, Nehemiah hit his own share of roadblocks. In fact, there was so much debris and rubble, it literally blocked his way (Neh. 2:14). Nehemiah faced a seemingly impossible situation. Not only was the wall around the city in ruins and its gates burned by fire, but wandering hearts and wayward faith had characterized the Israelites for generations. And these were the troops Nehemiah would have to rally in order to begin rebuilding.

Repairing the wall and the gates around Jerusalem was one of the most monumental rebuilding projects ever undertaken. Prior to making the necessary repairs, Nehemiah took time to carefully survey the damage that had occurred as a result of repeated attacks. He discreetly rode around Jerusalem (most likely by mule or donkey) to inspect the condition of each section, accurately noting what needed to be done.

I went to Jerusalem, and after staying there three days I set out during the night with a few others. I had not told anyone what my God had put in my heart to do for Jerusalem. There were no mounts with me except the one I was riding on.

By night I went out through the Valley Gate toward the Jackal Well and the Dung Gate, examining the walls of Jerusalem, which had been broken down, and its gates, which had been destroyed by fire. Then I moved on toward the Fountain Gate and the King's Pool, but there was not enough room for my mount to get through; so I went up the valley by night, examining the wall. Finally, I turned back and reentered through the Valley Gate. (Neh. 2:11–15)

Since Jerusalem was most often attacked from the north, some scholars say that Nehemiah only surveyed the southern section of the city because it was assumed the northern portion of the wall was completely destroyed. In addition, we can safely speculate that as Nehemiah surveyed the damage, he made important estimates as to the manpower, tools, and time it would take to complete the entire project. This is your charge as well.

Recognizing Your Roadblocks · *5:53 minutes*

Take an Honest Inventory

Like Nehemiah, one of the first things you need to do together is accurately survey the damage done to your relationship. To accomplish this, you must take an honest inventory to identify the roadblocks you're facing right now. But remember, you will not engage in this for the purpose of placing blame. Agree right now that you will not throw things from the past in each other's faces. Nothing will hinder your progress faster than trying to hurt each other with old offenses. In addition, ask God to broaden your perspective on your roadblocks through prayer, worship, and reading His Word. Most importantly, ask the Holy Spirit to help you take an unbiased look at your own heart as it relates to the matters at hand—past and present.

There are no shortcuts to real restoration. We often remind couples that reconciliation is a process, not a series of prescribed steps. More than following a recipe, reconciliation is about following Jesus Christ. Because God created every relationship to be unique, the specific methods He uses to repair one are not necessarily the methods He uses to repair another. However, one thing can be said of all relationships: honesty and humility are prerequisites for complete healing.

Be honest with God, yourself, and your spouse. This isn't the time to dance around difficult subjects to save face. Humbly admitting past mistakes stimulates mercy, not condemnation, even though you may fear the opposite is true (Prov. 28:13). The list of roadblocks we made at the dinner table didn't even include the down-and-dirty details of our blatant sins. That list would have taken up more than one sheet of paper. Suffice it to say, there were many strikes against us.

The restoration of your ruins is a time to get real with each other. Take a look at the way Nehemiah honestly described the state of Jerusalem's wall after he'd surveyed the damage: "Then I said to them, 'You see the trouble we are in: Jerusalem lies in ruins, and its gates have been burned with fire'" (Neh. 2:17). Notice that he didn't mince words, shrink back in despair, blame others, or become overwhelmed by what he was facing.

Remember, neither the destruction from your past nor the roadblocks you're facing are a surprise to God. He knows exactly what it's going to take to help your marriage grow into what He envisioned when He created it. For example, imagine our surprise when just moments before the first time we ever shared our testimony of reconciliation in public, I (Penny) noticed the person I'd had the affair with (at the end of our first marriage) was sitting in the audience. Clint and I were shell-shocked, but God wasn't. Instead of bailing out in fear, we whispered some reassuring words to each other, united our hearts, and shared our story anyway.

Past hurts and present-day trials will either divide you or draw you closer to God. If you're both growing closer to Him, then you can't help but grow closer to each other. Every time something like what we've just described happened (and there were many such incidents), we had an important choice to make. The same goes for you. Your choices, attitudes, actions, and behaviors regarding your trials and circumstances will either hinder true healing or propel you forward.

It is better to honestly acknowledge your roadblocks rather than sweep them under the rug. Take Scott and Cathy, for example. They were married on August 3, 1991. By their second year together, they had both accepted Christ and become involved in a local church. However, having God in their lives was no guarantee that their marriage would last. At the apex of their crisis, they'd been married just over eleven years and had three small children, ages six, four, and two. Solely for the sake of the kids, Scott and Cathy never physically separated, but they lived separate lives under the same roof for many months before they finally let down their defenses.

"Once we finally decided to make our marriage work, the first thing we *both* did was to take personal responsibility for our own actions. We had to intentionally take our eyes off each other and start changing the things we could change in our individual hearts. There was no more blaming or pointing fingers. It was time for both of us to own up to our part of the problem and let God make the first changes there."

Many of the problems in our first marriage occurred because neither of us was willing to admit our personal failures, nor were we totally honest with each other. We made critical mistakes by not revealing painful experiences from our pasts or owning up to our part of the problems we were facing. We kept various secrets from each other, and eventually those secrets—and the consequences of all our life experiences—subtly crawled out from under the carpet and crept in between us.

Remaining reconciled is a decision you make daily. It's not something that just happens once, after which you proceed to the next thing on your to-do list. No matter what lies ahead, you can be confident that greater than the task at hand is the great hand of God. In the next chapter, you'll discover that true wholeness and healing occur not so much from asking God to restore the shattered state of your relationship but in willingly asking Him to retool the state of your individual hearts. That's where the rebuilding really begins. In the words of Nehemiah to the Jewish leaders,

"Come, let us rebuild the wall of Jerusalem, and we will no longer be in disgrace." I also told them about the gracious hand of my God on me and what the king had said to me.

They replied, "Let us start rebuilding." So they began this good work. (Neh. 2:17–18)

Prayer to Overcome Obstacles

Father, reveal the changes You want to make in our individual hearts regarding our roadblocks. We willingly admit that we have sinned in our relationship with You and in our marriage. Begin Your work in us, and then show us how to overcome our obstacles. Help us discern the true nature of them and how You want us to navigate in each circumstance. Thoroughly examine our hearts, minds, and motives regarding the ways we can make positive changes in our relationship with You and each other. Where we've sinned, give us the courage to ask for forgiveness. Where we've wronged You or one another, grant us the desire to humbly apologize and repair these broken places. In the name of Jesus Christ we pray. Amen.

For a Marriage on the Mend

Take an Inventory

Take some time to pray together and ask God to identify the roadblocks you're currently facing in your marriage. Each spouse should make his or her own inventory list first. Then compare your lists. Identify the similarities and differences between the two. Combine your separate lists and bring each item to God in prayer on a weekly basis. Choose Scripture verses to guide you in navigating every obstacle. Pray those verses as promises over your roadblocks. Keep track of the movement you notice as God answers your prayers.

Questions to Consider

1. As you look over the inventory you created together, can you identify how each roadblock was initially erected?
2. Skim back over Nehemiah 1–2. List some of the oppositions Nehemiah faced when he first set out to rebuild the wall of Jerusalem. How did he overcome these difficulties, and how does this apply to your marriage?
3. What positive purposes might each roadblock serve in your relationship now?
4. What did you learn from making your inventory and comparing it to the one your spouse made? As you compared and combined your lists, what similarities and differences surprised you?

5. Are there any secrets or other experiences from your past that still need to be put on the table? If so, we suggest that you schedule a specific time together to pray and discuss these things. If necessary, consider having a trusted mentor, pastor, or counselor assist you with the process of disclosure.

6. Make sure you continue the process of adding positive and negative life events to your marriage timeline. Do you notice any roadblocks from the past that caused conflict?

Chapter 3

Forming a Firm Foundation

Although it was frustrating and downright scary to realize there weren't any resources available to guide us when we first reconciled, it forced us to immerse ourselves in God's Word. With our noses in our Bibles, we soon realized the obvious: God is no stranger to reconciliation. Everything we needed to heal our marriage could be found in His Word.

> Therefore, if anyone is in Christ, the new creation has come: The old has gone, the new is here! All this is from God, who reconciled us to himself through Christ and gave us the ministry of reconciliation: that God was reconciling the world to himself in Christ, not counting people's sins against them. And he has committed to us the message of reconciliation. We are therefore Christ's ambassadors, as though God were making his appeal through us. We implore you on Christ's behalf: Be reconciled to God. (2 Cor. 5:17–20)

Webster's Dictionary defines the word *reconciliation* as "the act of causing two people or groups to become friendly again after an argument or disagreement." In the passage from 2 Corinthians, the Bible indicates that God desires reconciliation between Himself and

His people. Reconciliation was perfectly modeled when God sent His Son to forgive us and cleanse us from sin (Rom. 5:10–11). God's Word also says that He desires reconciled relationships between all believers (Matt. 5:23–24). Reestablishing relationships in need of healing clearly occupies God's heart.

The two most important things these passages on reconciliation reveal are that (1) God wants us to focus on maintaining a reconciled relationship with Him *first*, before we concern ourselves with each other, and (2) reconciliation takes action on the part of both parties involved.

Carl and Caren learned these truths the hard way. "The first ten years of our relationship were very rough. Eventually, our struggles took their toll and we filed for divorce. In one final attempt to save our marriage, we attended a weekend retreat, even though neither of us wanted to go. We thank God for working through the retreat speakers to bring us the exact message of conviction and hope we needed to hear. In the hotel lobby, we knelt down in prayer; asking Jesus into our hearts and giving Him full command over our lives. We asked for God's forgiveness and His strength to help us build a marriage that would bring Him honor and glory.

"Every day since then, we've thanked God for the crisis and pain we went through because that's what brought us to the place of complete brokenness before our holy God. All the pride, bitterness, anger—everything we were both carrying around—was the bondage that had kept us from experiencing the life God had planned.

"It was our crisis that made us realize our true need for Jesus. Without Christ at the center of our lives and our marriage, we would only end up in captivity. In the grip of God's grace and in His perfect timing, we finally came to realize that our struggles were more about what God wanted to teach us about ourselves and Him than about getting what we wanted out of our marriage."

Carl and Caren aren't alone. Many couples fall into the trap of leaving God out of their marriage. In addition, they point fingers at each other's faults, falsely assuming the relationship can only be restored if the *other* person changes. But God's first priority is *your* heart. Deal with that and your marriage will naturally improve.

In our own relationship, God's ways of mending it have consistently gone far beyond what either of us could have comprehended. We still exchange glances of disbelief over what God has done to reconcile and restore us. For many years after our divorce, we had both run from God, though neither of us knew it about the other because we had neither seen nor heard from each other after we parted. Not until we focused on our individual relationships with God did He reconnect us.

For me (Penny), eight years passed after I left Clint before I finally focused my life on God and stopped resisting Him. I vividly remember the night I stretched out my arms, admitted my sins, and asked God to forgive me. After that, I set my entire life and every priority on deepening my relationship with Him through prayer, reading the Bible, worship, and learning from mature believers. I also committed to reconciling the relationships I'd broken. Of course, I *never* planned to contact Clint—the thought was too overwhelming. But through God's unconditional love and the kindness of believers He placed in my life, the Holy Spirit urged me to take a leap of faith and write Clint an apology letter.

My intention was to tell Clint the truth about what I'd done all those years ago, ask his forgiveness, and bring closure to that part of my past. Most importantly, I wanted to obey God and what His Word said about relationships. So one chilly February night in 2002, I located Clint's address via the Internet and was stunned to discover he was living more than three thousand miles away in Florida. That night, I wrote the most honest letter

I could, never dreaming it would result in our remarriage just six months later.

Whatever intricate and intimate details your own marriage crisis may involve, focus first on daily reconciling your individual relationships with God. Then allow Him to guide you in the restoration of your marriage. Your individual relationships with God must be the foundation of your marriage. Before you begin seeking God about His plan for your marriage, you must each ask Him about His plan for your heart. Whether you're a new believer or have been a Christian for many years, your heart will always remain God's top priority.

Laying the Groundwork

When we were married the first time, we spent all our time doing things for God instead of spending time alone with Him. If something needed to be done at church, Penny and I were the first to respond. We were the little "church darlings," if you will, and proud of it. While I was busy teaching Sunday school and helping with various projects around the church, Penny was singing in the choir, leading vacation Bible school, and serving as the deacon of missions. Not only was all our free time tied up at church, but we were each serving in different areas. As a result, we rarely worshipped together or spent quality time with other Christian couples; we had exchanged intimate relationships with God and each other for dutiful service to our church and the accolades that came with it. This perched us for quite a fall. Our actions appeared noble, but a wedge of pride lodged between us that would eventually split us apart.

The same thing is happening today in countless other marriages. Church is vital to the lives of believers and to God's purposes on earth. However, hurting couples are slipping in epidemic numbers through the cracks in the church pews or hiding behind ministry commitments while their marriages are crumbling. Why? Because church involvement is not the same as a relationship with God—and it can never be a substitute.

When couples contact us for help, we begin by asking, "Tell us about your walk with God." Most people give us a blank look, as if to say, "What does *that* have to do with my marriage? I want to talk to you about my spouse."

Many people fail to see the correlation between the quality of their relationship with God and their marriage. We too were once blind to that connection. But during our years apart, each of us developed the deep spiritual roots we hadn't put down as young converts. And God showed us how the intimacy we cultivated with Him directly affected everything else in our lives, especially our relationships.

Before you go any further, take a moment to do a self-assessment of your personal relationship with God. How would you characterize it? Check the statement that best applies.

- -
Spiritual Self-Assessment
- -

____ Spending time with God in prayer, Bible reading, worship, and fellowship is a high priority in my life each day.

____ At least three or four times a week, I spend time reading God's Word and praying.

____ I seldom spend time alone with God.

____ I do not have a personal relationship with God. (If you marked this statement, it's important to speak with a mature Christian or a pastor about how to have a personal relationship with God.)

If you know that your personal relationship with God is not where it should be, don't berate yourself. Your inadequacy will be met by God's sufficiency as you open this area of your life to His healing.

The State of Your Heart

As we look again at the book of Nehemiah as the guide for restoration, we see that this man knew the correlation between intimacy
with God and relationships with others.

> When I heard these things, I sat down and wept. For some
> days I mourned and fasted and prayed before the God of
> heaven. Then I said: "LORD, the God of heaven, the great and
> awesome God, who keeps his covenant of love with those
> who love him and keep his commands, let your ear be atten-
> tive and your eyes open to hear the prayer your servant is
> praying before you day and night for your servants, the peo-
> ple of Israel." (Neh. 1:4–6)

Nehemiah had a personal relationship with God. He knew God
and His commands. He understood the truth about who God was
and what He desired for the complete restoration of His covenant
with the Israelites. Nehemiah also realized the odds were stacked
against his being able to restore Jerusalem and reform its people.

Similarly, the odds were stacked against our restoration as a couple. They're stacked against yours too. But God doesn't need favorable odds. He's God. Give Him your whole heart and spend time
with Him. Learn as much from His Word about relationships as you
possibly can. Do these things and healing will happen.

Daily, intentional intimacy with God is essential. After we remarried, we soon realized that, if anything, our individual time with
God should increase, not decrease. Most couples do just the opposite. Instead, you should make a conscious decision each day to
nurture your relationship with God first, and then to nurture your
mate. We make a point of having little interaction with each other
in the morning until we've both spent time in the Word and prayer.
Things seem to run much better that way.

All marital dysfunction can be traced back to the soul's deep desire for love and our misguided attempts to find it. Your God-given ache for love can only be satisfied by Him. When you allow God to fill your heart with His love and meet all your needs each day, you'll have an abundance of love to give away. Additionally, the forms that love takes will be pure and holy. As He pours into you, you'll pour into others. The opposite is also true: if you don't spend time receiving His love and allowing Him to meet your deepest needs, you cannot love others or meet their needs.

Spending time with God sounds simple. But there are many demands calling for your time and attention, such as family, work, school, and church. Although these things are extremely important, they can easily crowd out your time with God. If your individual relationship with Him is not in alignment with the Word, then the rest of your relationships and responsibilities will suffer.

Going Deeper with God

There are several ways you can nurture intimacy with God. Since time is a scarce commodity in today's families, it's essential that you learn how to maximize your time with Him. Take a look at the list below and place a check mark next to the spiritual disciplines you engage in on a regular basis. If you're not meeting with God daily, place a check mark next to the things you would like to implement.

- -
Spiritual Disciplines
- -

___ Reading the Bible
___ Memorizing Scripture verses
___ Prayer
___ Journaling
___ Worship

There are various ways you can organize your daily time with God. Many people refer to this time as their "quiet time." Neither of us understood what a quiet time entailed when we first became Christians; we got caught in a legalistic mind-set, viewing God more as a taskmaster and a distant authority figure than as the Grand Lover who longed to be with us. But we eventually discovered that there are many ways to nurture greater intimacy with God.

Forming a Firm Foundation, for Men · *6:29 minutes*

Forming a Firm Foundation, for Women · *4:06 minutes*

Consistency is key. Urgent matters often threaten to get in the way of spending time with God, but that's all the more reason to prioritize that time. If you're not spending consistent time with God, start with what we call the "10/10/10 Plan" to jumpstart your relationship. The idea is simple: each day, spend ten minutes reading the Bible, ten minutes journaling in response to what you read, and ten minutes talking and listening to God through prayer.

There are no rules for the way you spend time with God, except that you should regularly engage in the disciplines His Word emphasizes. However, some people do better having a model to follow. The 10/10/10 Plan is a simple way to structure your quiet time. Once you've used it consistently for several weeks, consider other approaches as well as increasing your time with Him.

As with any relationship, the more your love and intimacy develop and deepen, the more you'll desire to spend time with God. Work toward giving Him an appropriate tithe (ten percent) of your time. For example, if you're awake for sixteen hours each day, that would equal spending a little over an hour and a half with God. (This time doesn't always have to occur in one sitting.)

Here are the tools we use in our own quiet times to deepen our intimacy with God and build a lasting foundation for our marriage.

Read the Bible

Let's start with the obvious. It's impossible to discover God's will for your life if you don't read the Bible consistently. Your marriage doesn't have a chance of making it if you aren't willing to commit time to understanding the ways God intended it to function. Even reading a psalm or a proverb each day will make a significant difference in your life and your relationship with your spouse.

If you need a more structured approach to reading, there are various Bible reading plans available on the Internet. Many are designed to help you read through the entire Bible in one year. There are also several one-year Bibles you can purchase at your local Christian bookstore or online bookseller.

Everyone is different. An honorable goal is to read the Word in a way that reflects your unique relationship with God. What's important in your Bible reading isn't its quantity (how much you read) but its quality (how you read it and apply it to your life).

Memorize Scripture · *5:02 minutes*

Memorize Scripture

Memorizing Bible verses isn't just for children. It's definitely for adults—and for you. Now more than ever, you need to have God's promises hidden in your heart and ready on the tip of your tongue. Start slowly. Select one verse to memorize each week. Ask God for the verses He wants you to memorize.

To help you memorize Scripture, write the verses onto index cards and place them in several prominent locations around your workplace and/or home. Laminating these cards will make them more durable. Pray through the verse(s) as you go through the week so they become a part of your dialogue back to God. For example:

Memory Verse: "And my God will meet all your needs according to the riches of his glory in Christ Jesus" (Phil. 4:19).

Prayer Dialogue: "God, I believe You will meet all my needs, and I rely on You to do so today in every area of my life."

The more you practice this, the more comfortable and natural it will become. Praying your memory verse(s) back to God is a powerful way to communicate your trust in Him. Because His Word is alive and active, your prayers will stir the Holy Spirit, and you'll become more steadfast and resilient when challenges arise.

Choose verses that are meaningful to you. If you are unfamiliar with the Bible, here are a few suggestions to get you started:

· "But seek first his kingdom and his righteousness, and all these things will be given to you as well" (Matt. 6:33).
· "I can do all this through him who gives me strength" (Phil. 4:13).
· "I have told you these things, so that in me you may have peace. In this world you will have trouble. But take heart! I have overcome the world" (John 16:33).

- "For God so loved the world that he gave his one and only Son, that whoever believes in him shall not perish but have eternal life" (John 3:16).
- "Cast all your anxiety on him because he cares for you" (1 Peter 5:7).
- "Love the LORD your God with all your heart and with all your soul and with all your strength" (Deut. 6:5).

Pray Often

Prayer is so essential to maintaining reconciled relationships that we've devoted a whole chapter to it (see chapter 8). However, we'll briefly state a few basics here. One simple principle we've incorporated into our marriage is, we don't leave the house in the morning until we've spent two or three minutes praying together. A few minutes doesn't seem like much, but God has honored our commitment. Praying together each morning instills a sense of God's complete control and sovereignty over our marriage.

Many people maintain a prayer list or prayer journal to remind them of the people and circumstances they're praying for and to help develop a more complete prayer life. At times, we change up our prayer lives to keep our conversations with God fresh. Sometimes we use a prayer list; sometimes we toss the list aside and pray as the Holy Spirit leads. Both of us keep a prayer journal as a way of tracing God's hand.

Keeping a prayer list may seem overwhelming at times. One helpful approach is to arrange it into a daily format. For example:

- -
My Prayer List
- -

Monday – Pray for your spouse, marriage, and family.
Tuesday – Pray for your friends.

Wednesday – Pray for your pastors and your church.
Thursday – Pray for your coworkers, classmates, etc.
Friday – Pray for the unsaved people in your life.
Saturday – Pray for world leaders, missionaries, and global
   concerns.
Sunday – Give thanks to God in prayer for all the blessings
   He's bestowed upon you.

If you use a format such as the one written above, we suggest that you pray for your marriage every day, not just once a week.

It takes time to develop an impulse to pray at all times. But eventually, prayer can become as automatic and necessary as breathing. Make that your goal. You learn to pray by praying and praying and praying again.

Keep a Personal Journal

Penny and I have kept journals for years. When we first reconciled, sharing past journal entries was a powerful way to see how God had divinely orchestrated our intersection.

Women use journaling more often than men. So I tell guys how God changed me from being a man who didn't like to write anything to one who can't go a day without opening his journal to write. My journal is reserved solely for intercession; my mind wanders less during prayer if I write down my requests. In my journal, I pray about my relationship with God, Penny, and concerns related to our family, friends, and ministry. I also express praise to God for answers to prayer.

Penny uses her journal to convey her feelings and thoughts to God. In it, she responds to His Word, our marriage, family, friends, and other events that transpire. As of this writing, she's filled more than fifty journals which span approximately thirty-five years.

Keep a Personal Journal, for Women · *4:04 minutes*

 Keep a Personal Journal, for Men · *8:38 minutes*

Journal in whatever way suits you best. We've developed a simple framework as a starting point.

Journal Framework

Record a verse(s) from your Bible reading time.
Relate that verse to your own life.
Respond to God by writing a prayer.
Rejoice and give thanks to God for something.

Here is one example of what this framework might look like in your journal:

Record: "I consider that our present sufferings are not worth comparing with the glory that will be revealed in us" (Rom. 8:18).
Relate: When I get busy during the day and trials come, I forget that what I'm dealing with is nothing compared to what I can look forward to when I spend eternity in heaven with God.
Respond: Father, please remind me that I have an eternal hope to anticipate. When challenges come, may I remember that my struggles have a divine purpose. In Jesus' name I pray. Amen.

Rejoice: I'm grateful for Your Word. You are always faithful to hear my prayers and keep Your promises. Thank You for being patient with me.

If you want your journal time to be less structured and more open-ended, consider using some of these journal prompts:

I just wanted to take a moment to say . . .
I'm concerned about what I should do regarding . . .
I want to thank You for . . .
What do You think about . . . ?
Do You think I should . . . ?
I'm sorry for . . .
I was wondering if . . .
One of the things I appreciate about Your love is . . .
If I could see You face-to-face right now, I would . . .
I've been reluctant to . . .
I commit to You that I will . . .
I confess my sins of . . .

Worship God

Many people think worship is something that only takes place at church or in a large group setting. But you can worship God in many ways all by yourself. Worshipping God means you're putting Him in His rightful place—lifted up and magnified. Worship causes an immediate shift in your perspective. Worship can take many forms because it includes anything that gives God glory, such as singing, reading Scripture aloud, or listening to music that exalts Him. Like prayer, worship can be done anytime and anywhere, because it is an attitude of your heart reflected in everything you do.

I (Penny) love my private worship time: to be shut away from

others and totally alone with God to express my love and gratitude to Him. When duty calls, I ask God to help me worship Him
through my responsibilities and activities. Even the most mundane
tasks can be transformed into a form of worship. When praising
God is the attitude and intent of your heart, you can worship Him
no matter where you are or what you're doing. As with developing
your prayer life, developing creative ways to worship God takes time
and practice.

In Hot Pursuit

When you met and fell in love with your spouse, a pursuit ensued.
You courted each other and spent time getting to know one another's history, dislikes, desires, and dreams. You invested in becoming
a part of each other's lives because you were in love. That's how you
should pursue God. Court Him. Date Him. Study Him. Spend time
getting to know His Word, His history with humankind, His miracles, His dislikes, and His desires.

Always focus on God first and foremost. When marital conflicts
arise, the tendency is to focus on your spouse or on the crisis. But
God wants you to seek Him first and let Him be in charge of everything else (Matt. 6:33). As you spend time with God and become
a willing participant in the processes He's using to make you
holy, positive changes will occur in your heart regardless of your
circumstances.

If you're not spending time in the Word and in prayer each day, it
will be impossible to see significant changes in your marriage. Now
more than ever, buckle down and spend quality time with Him. One
suggestion: take whatever time you're spending with God right now
and, in a step of faith, double it for the next forty days. Give God
a double portion and expect Him to honor your efforts out of His
grace.

Prayer to Form a Firm Foundation

Father, we want to deepen our knowledge of You. Part of the reason we're going through trials in our relationship is that You want to get our attention and teach us something about who You are. But we don't quite know how to begin pursuing You, so we're asking You to extend and deepen the time we're spending with You each day. Show us how to lay a firm foundation. Teach us how to spend quality time with You in a way that keeps us in the center of Your will. Help us incorporate new ideas, and teach us how to make this practice more of a priority.

For a Marriage on the Mend

Making a Connection

Pursuing God's presence is something you'll do for the rest of your life. It's important to ask other Christians what they do to nurture spiritual intimacy. Between now and next week, ask one or two people what they do to deepen their relationship with God. Share your discoveries with your spouse.

Questions to Consider

1. Did any ideas for spiritual disciplines or quiet times spark your interest or curiosity? Share them with your spouse.
2. Read Nehemiah 3 and 4. What specific progress is made on the rebuilding of Jerusalem's wall, and what problems does Nehemiah encounter?
3. What is one discipline you'll consider trying in your relationship with God this week? Share your plans with a trusted friend, and ask him or her to pray for your quiet time during the coming week.

4. Take out your marriage timeline and add any spiritual life events to it. Positive spiritual events may include things such as the salvation of a family member, baptisms, or finding a new home church. Negative spiritual life events might include the loss of a loved one, a crisis of faith, or a conflict that upset you and/or other members of your church.

Chapter 4

Building Bridges of Forgiveness and Faith

Our ministry makes us acutely aware of the widespread havoc divorce is wreaking across all racial, educational, socioeconomic, and denominational boundaries. Satan is serving up marriages and families on a skewer, and it's tearing our world apart. In South Carolina, a bitter marital battle ended in 2014 when a father murdered his five children after divorcing their mother for having an affair. It wasn't the first such incident, and it won't be the last.

Before working with troubled marriages, we served as public school teachers. Each day we witnessed the fallout of marital dysfunction on the faces of our students. Within the first few days of school, it was easy to tell which students were living with both parents and which students weren't. On every continent, battles between spouses are leaving countless wounded children in their wake. We look upon the devastation and the way it's impacting this generation—as well as the threat it poses for the next—and our hearts break.

God's heart is breaking too.

What's most tragic is that spouses are fighting the wrong opponent. They are warring against themselves, each other, and their children instead of fighting the real enemy, Satan. Let us give you another vivid example.

A husband who has been hiding his addiction to pornography is finally caught in the act by his wife. Her discovery brings an onslaught of rage: "How could you do this to me? To our family?"

Her head is spinning. Distraught, she storms out of the house and formulates a plan to leave him. In the back of her mind, she's already decided that divorce is her *only* option. In a single moment, her whole world has turned upside down. She's reeling—and it's all *his* fault.

"I'll never forgive him!"

Disgusted, hurt, and betrayed, she rises up against her husband. Understandably so.

For years, the husband feared his wife would discover his secret. Now she knows. Shame sickens his gut. Running through his mind are all the things he stands to lose.

"What have I done?" Unworthiness overtakes him and he begins to sob. He has resolved to stop surfing the Internet and looking at porn thousands of times, but he just can't seem to quit.

"What's wrong with me?" he cries. Confused and repulsed by the man he's become, he rises up against himself.

Maybe this scenario hits close to home for you. Or perhaps it wasn't an addiction that tore your marriage in two, but another person. Fidelity was never intended to be a mere fantasy or lofty ideal, yet sadly, mutual faithfulness in marriage has become something of a rarity. Some people have even abandoned their spouse for a same-sex relationship. Regardless of the details of the infidelity, the faithful spouse is left to deal with an unbearable betrayal.

In still other marriages, infidelity isn't the issue. Rather, a series of problems and chronic arguing have finally taken their toll.

No matter what the circumstances—family drama, debt, addiction, infidelity, or rebellion—everyone who comes to us has been cut to the core in their relationship. And all have one thing in common: an unmet need for true intimacy and unconditional love that has been lodged in our DNA since the fall of humanity. Marital breakdown is just a manifestation of that unmet need.

Let's be honest. At one level or another, every one of us is trying to fill legitimate needs with counterfeit solutions. It's the Enemy's most underhanded weapon, and it's tearing at the fabric of our very existence. We don't wish to split theological or psychological hairs over why people do the things they do; there are counselors, professors, pastors, and scholars who can speak to these matters far better than we can. Our intention is simply to set the stage for thought-provoking and potentially relationship-transforming questions.

What would happen if the wife described earlier rose up against the real Enemy instead of her husband? What if her husband stopped condemning himself or anyone else for his problems and, instead, placed blame where blame belonged and sought help? And what if both parties, broken and humbled before God, confessed their individual part in the breakdown of the marriage, received God's forgiveness, extended forgiveness to one another, and pursued true healing?

What if you and your spouse did the same thing?

We're not saying that sinful behavior should be shrugged off or glossed over. By no means: sin is sin, and it must be dealt with. Those who have indulged in inappropriate self-gratification at any level must deal with the consequences. But all outward manifestations of marital division have, as their source, a wound that runs much deeper. It is an ache that has long been gravely misunderstood. And until its true source is unveiled and addressed, the heights of intimacy and restoration in your marriage will fall far short of what God intends.

What is this great ache gnawing at our hearts? Proverbs 19:22 says it best: "What a person desires is unfailing love." Much of the rest of the Bible demonstrates undeniably that human beings will do just about anything to be loved.

That was certainly true for Penny and me. Relationships, material possessions, sex, academic pursuits, career achievements, food—between the two of us, we tried many remedies in search of the one thing that would soothe the ache in our souls. All of our attempts to find love failed—except one. Years of pining after lesser lovers resulted in the discovery that *nothing* on earth could fill the God-sized void in our hearts. Only God can do that, and nothing else could ever take His rightful place.

 Building Bridges of Forgiveness and Faith · *6:03 minutes*

Learning to Forgive

Penny and I rarely go into specific detail about our breakup; however, Penny does share that she was unfaithful at the end of our first marriage, and I admit the ways my tough-guy personality contributed to our divorce. After our speaking engagements, men often ask me, "Clint, how could you ever forgive Penny for what she did?" Sometimes they'll tell me about their own wives' affairs or something else their wives did that was "absolutely unforgivable."

My response is always the same: "How could I *not* forgive Penny?" During the years we were apart, I finally came to an important understanding. Although I'm entitled to nothing, Christ has given me everything. He forgave *all* my sins, and He asks me to do the same where others are concerned. That includes forgiving Penny.

When I first accepted Christ as my Savior in 1981, I knew about

God's forgiveness, but it wasn't until many years later that I really understood the magnitude of what Jesus did on the cross to pardon my sins—including my marital sins. While I wasn't unfaithful to Penny, there were still many things I'd done wrong. I needed to ask Penny's forgiveness for those things, just as she did with me.

I forgave Penny years before I ever received her letter asking for forgiveness. But what I did was nothing noble. Forgiveness is part of the cross we are to bear as disciples. It is our obligation to pursue and extend forgiveness, no matter what the offense or the cost. Forgiveness is a process. Sometimes it happens overnight, but usually it takes work, time, and effort, especially where betrayal is concerned.

Women tend to be less reluctant than men when it comes to saying, "I'm sorry. Will you please forgive me?" Guys, it's time to make a change. Taking the initiative to apologize when conflicts arise is your spiritual responsibility. If you want your wife to respect your leadership, you must nurture their respect by being man enough to say, "I'm sorry for my part of the problem. Please forgive me." Nothing melts the tension faster than humbly apologizing and asking for forgiveness.

Nehemiah perfectly reflects this. He was willing to take full responsibility for acknowledging and identifying himself as a part of the problem during his attempts to reform the Israelites and rebuild Jerusalem.

> "I confess the sins we Israelites, including myself and my father's family, have committed against you. We have acted very wickedly toward you. We have not obeyed the commands, decrees and laws you gave your servant Moses." (Neh. 1:6–7)

Nehemiah wasn't quick to point the finger at others as he petitioned God. Instead, he admitted his own sinful nature as a part of what needed redemption. *"We* have acted very wickedly" and *"we* have not obeyed," he said as he stood before God (emphasis added).

Nehemiah was also aware of the wicked acts committed against God in past generations. Generational sin can subtly permeate the lineage of a family for years without being detected. It seethes beneath the surface of our awareness, poisoning our spiritual freedom. Nehemiah addressed the issue, taking responsibility by privately and publicly confessing the sins of his forefathers.

We can't engage in confession, repentance, and forgiveness often enough. Honest confession and repentance of our shortcomings are ongoing parts of nurturing a lifestyle of forgiveness and reconciliation that permeates all of our relationships. Many of the problems in marriages today are a result of pride and an unwillingness to own up to mistakes and sins—both past and present.

What's the Difference?

This chapter focuses on combining forgiveness and faith to build bridges of reconciliation over your past. Let's start by clarifying the difference between *forgiveness* and *reconciliation*. The simplest explanation is this: it only takes one party to *forgive* an offense or ask for forgiveness, but it takes two parties to *reconcile* a relationship. For example, I forgave Penny on my own, but our marriage wasn't reconciled until we *both* came together and made the decision to reestablish our relationship.

During His ministry on earth, Jesus modeled forgiveness and reconciliation in numerous ways. You can see examples throughout the Gospels as He responded to relationships in crisis. Unfortunately, the ways of the world run directly counter to forgiveness and reconciliation. Satan loves nothing more than to drive a wedge between believers. He does so primarily through unforgiveness, which breaks down relationships more swiftly than anything else.

Couples who have passed through an initial crisis must constantly be aware of the subtle ways the Enemy will attempt to divert them from a closer relationship with God and each other by harboring unforgiveness. Immediately after we remarried, Penny and I experienced the Enemy's desire to use what had happened in our pasts to divide and conquer us. His first assault came on our wedding day.

Our remarriage ceremony and reception were wonderful. We were surrounded by family, friends, and colleagues. Even some of the people who were present at our first wedding came to celebrate with us. Penny was beside herself with joy the entire night. That's not to say I wasn't, but most of the people at our wedding were much more important in her life during our years apart, since I had moved to Florida. Naturally, Penny wanted to spend as much time with her family and friends as possible. But like most guys, I had other things on my mind. After a few hours of celebrating, I was ready to begin our first night together after eleven long years apart.

But it seemed that the readier I was to go, the more content Penny was to stay. As I observed her celebrating with friends and colleagues—people with whom I was barely acquainted—one of her friends from church walked up to me, leaned in front of my face, and threatened, "Hey, bud, make sure you don't mess this up."

Caught off-guard, I just smiled and nodded at the guy, but inside my anger was brewing. We'd only been married a few hours, and I didn't need that kind of pressure. While I didn't realize it at the time, I was not only feeling the stress of the present, but something had triggered failure from the past as well.

It seemed to take Penny forever to say all her goodbyes. I knew that if she'd had her way, we would have stayed at the reception for a few more hours. Her friend's words of caution burned inside me, but I didn't tell Penny what happened or how I was feeling. When we finally got in the car to leave, the tension had mounted. We exchanged few words on the drive back to the house.

We managed to overcome this problem and enjoy our first night back together as husband and wife. But after this experience, we realized that dealing rationally and appropriately with our painful memories (as well as new challenges) would take some serious effort.

Later we discussed what happened, and during our conversation, I discovered that Penny was having her own upsurge of pain from the past. She explained the ways she felt I was subtly trying to control her by being silent yet visibly aggravated when she wanted to stay at the reception. For Penny, my attitude stirred up old memories of the conflicts that occurred at the end of our first marriage when I would shut down and stop communicating.

 Building Bridges over Unpleasant Memories • *7:08 minutes*

Building Bridges over Unpleasant Memories

We refer to these uncomfortable experiences as *traumatic triggers*. A traumatic trigger is an unpleasant memory that unexpectedly surfaces and sucks the life out of your relationship. All conflicted couples experience these moments, and you will too if you haven't already. The way you handle these triggers can make or break you.

When painful or fearful memories are triggered, it feels as if the breath from your chest is being sucked out with a high-powered vacuum. These rushes of pain and fear are ripe with the potential for unforgiveness to subtly creep in and drive a wedge between you. Therefore it is important to recognize these events while they're happening and pray for healthy ways to cope with them.

Dick and Joni, a couple we met several years ago, experienced many traumatic triggers during their process of restoration. "At the beginning of our crisis, old triggers would come minute by minute," Joni honestly admitted. "Through those experiences, we learned that we must keep our armor on (Eph. 6:11) and hold every thought captive to the obedience of Christ (2 Cor. 10:5).

"Individually, we would immediately pray about trigger thoughts and lay them at the foot of the cross, realizing they're based on fear that seeks to steal, kill, and destroy. Usually the thought is quickly crushed by God's truth. But if it lingers, we share it with each other and pray together. We still work on not getting offended by one another's worries, fears, or negative thoughts and on not allowing triggers to take us back to the guilt and shame of our past."

Dick continued, "Love is a risk, but we've decided it's a risk worth taking. We've removed the word 'divorce' from our vocabulary and committed to investing time and effort to grow together instead of apart. Each day, our energies are put into fighting for our marriage and building a legacy for our children. Never forget your marriage is worth saving."

To understand traumatic triggers and the ways you can pro-actively and effectively use them to draw closer together, imagine you are both standing at the bank of a rushing river. The river represents the pain, dissension, fear, betrayal, and sins of the past. The waters appear dark, murky, and impossible to cross. If you attempt to wade through the river, you'll be swept up in the current, sucked under, and drowned. But you have to get to the other side of the river to continue your journey together. You need a bridge to stretch over these treacherous waters. Forgiveness and faith are your bridge builders.

Combined with prayer, forgiveness and faith will build a bridge strong enough to carry you safely to the other side. When a painful event or memory is triggered, you must recognize what is happening, forgive the offense, and take a step of faith, whatever that looks like at the time. Sometimes, asking God and your spouse for forgiveness turns out to be the greatest step of faith required to get over a triggered memory. At other times, extending forgiveness to your spouse, or perhaps someone else, is the faith God requires.

The last six chapters of Nehemiah focus on reform—transforming Israel's painful past into a promising future. Like you, Nehemiah stood on the banks of some pretty murky waters, and he needed a sturdy bridge to get to the other side. Generations of sin and rebellion had ravaged the nation and almost swept it off the map.

> But they, our ancestors, became arrogant and stiff-necked, and they did not obey your commands. They refused to listen and failed to remember the miracles you performed among them. They became stiff-necked and in their rebellion appointed a leader in order to return to their slavery. (Neh. 9:16–17)

But Nehemiah knew how to build a bridge over Israel's sinful past with forgiveness and faith. He recognized that God had—and still has—a long history of bridge building.

> But you are a forgiving God, gracious and compassionate, slow to anger and abounding in love. Therefore you did not desert them, even when they cast for themselves an image of a calf and said, 'This is your god, who brought you up out of Egypt,' or when they committed awful blasphemies. (Neh. 9:17–18)

Effectively dealing with traumatic triggers is an ongoing process that takes practice, but they can be completely overcome through forgiveness and faith. Better yet, these experiences can serve as catalysts for a stronger relationship. One of the benefits of building bridges together is that your perspectives on the past change and increasingly unite. When you stand on a bridge and look down, that higher vantage point allows both of you to look more objectively and clearly at your surroundings and circumstances and rise together above the very things that took your marriage down in the first place.

When we first saw Scott and Sylvia together, we were taken in by the affectionate demeanor between them. What we didn't realize was that, after fourteen years of marriage and raising three children, they were barely on the other side of a major crisis.

"There are nineteen divorces within our extended families, and we don't want to end up being divorce number twenty," Sylvia said.

Once we got to know them, they entrusted more of their marriage story to us. We could sense their pain as they shared about the traumatic triggers they were still experiencing and how those moments seemed to be hindering their progress toward healing.

Sylvia said, "It seems like every time I turn around, I'm faced with another memory of what happened, and I immediately feel bitter toward Scott."

"Frankly, I don't know what to do when this happens," said Scott. "I can see the bitterness come over Sylvia, and once again I'm full of remorse and shame, because I know my actions hurt her—and are still hurting her."

Over the next several months, we met with Scott and Sylvia over dinner and talked about the difficulties they were experiencing. As a result of their commitment to remain reconciled and deepen their individual relationships with God, they began tackling *every* traumatic trigger together in prayer, no matter how painful. Scott and Sylvia intentionally pursued seeking and extending forgiveness and asked God for the faith to move forward. In addition, when something triggered pain from the past, each of them asked Him this key question: "God, how do You want to change *my* heart through this pain?"

The Heart of Reconciliation

The Heart of Reconciliation, Part 1 • *7:56 minutes*

No matter who is responsible for whatever transpired in your marriage, God wants to work in *your* heart. When people ask us exactly how to reconcile with their spouse, we explain that it's much more about the heart than the how.

God wants to make a change in your heart, and appropriately handling a traumatic trigger is one of the most effective ways He will accomplish this. Let God help you foster a spirit of reconciliation and forgiveness, especially if your spouse has committed offenses that continue to threaten faith's forward motion.

There are ten heart attitudes that will help you build sturdy bridges of forgiveness and faith and let go of the past. Cultivating these attitudes will lead you to freedom. They will also serve as the support structure for the new bridges of faith you'll build together. Each attitude is of equal importance.

1. Be Prayerful. Spend as much time as possible in prayer regarding the traumatic triggers in your marriage. Conflict often arises from these experiences when you point the finger at your spouse's faults or use things from the past against him or her. Instead, direct your hands and heart to God in prayer. If necessary, find a confidential prayer partner who will support you. (More information about prayer partners is included in chapter 10.) When you sense a traumatic trigger occurring, reach out to your spouse and/or prayer partner. Pray instead of pulling away.

2. Be Mindful. Fostering and maintaining a healthy marriage requires a conscious choice to cultivate a mind-set of loyalty and devotion amid turbulent waters. When a relationship isn't satisfying, it's tempting to seek pleasure elsewhere. No matter how you might feel, the arms of another person, spending large sums of money, drinking excessively, indulging in pornography, eating uncontrollably, or confiding in a person of the opposite sex will not bring you lasting satisfaction. Make a conscious decision to remain faithful to God and your spouse in all areas of your life. Spend your time wisely by coping with difficulties in biblical ways.

3. Be Grateful. Praising and worshipping God in the midst of your pain refocuses your attention on Him and ushers true healing into your heart and mind. Go out of your way to extend gratitude to your spouse. Instead of focusing on your frustration, engage in a labor of love and service for your mate. Worship God with your hands up. Wait for God with your hands open. And work for God with your hands out.

4. Be Approachable. Let down your defenses. Encourage your spouse to come to you when a traumatic trigger gets activated. Be open to hearing your spouse's opinions and feelings. Validate the pain and emotion he or she is experiencing by listening and asking clarifying questions. Listen more. Talk less. Welcome the expression of your mate's feelings, as difficult as it may be to hear them. Be aware of your body language at all times. Suspend judgment. Extend mercy.

5. Be Resourceful. If necessary, know when and where to get extra help to deal with past offenses. Sometimes it's advisable to seek out additional resources to get you over a particular hurdle. Utilize the wisdom and counsel of other Christians, mentors, pastors, counselors, support providers, and healthcare professionals. Seek advice and mentoring from a couple who has also overcome obstacles.

The Heart of Reconciliation, Part 2 · *6:59 minutes*

6. Be Humble. Humility is a necessary prerequisite for extending and receiving forgiveness. It indicates that you have an accurate view of who God is, who you are, and who you are becoming. Humility requires complete honesty. It's never easy to admit your mistakes or secrets, but humility and honesty stimulate mercy. Dancing around the subject because of pride or dishonesty may save face, but it will hinder true healing.

7. Be Careful. Avoid making assumptions or judgments about your spouse's motives, attitudes, or behaviors. Ask God to reveal any ways *you* are setting up roadblocks or harboring unforgiveness. Choose appropriate times to discuss traumatic triggers (not in the heat of the moment, late at night, or when others are present). Your spouse is precious to God. Treat his or her feelings and fears with respect and dignity, even if you don't understand them.

8. Be Practical. Make the most of every opportunity to practice, pursue, and seek forgiveness. Ask God for practical passages of Scripture to help you overcome each traumatic trigger. Write the passages into prayers. When you're hurt, discouraged, or frustrated, get those Scripture passages out and read them aloud to God. Spend time writing down your feelings and fears in a journal.

9. Be Respectful. Respect and honor the process and timing God is using in your marriage, even though it feels uncomfortable. Every relationship is different and so is every traumatic trigger. The way

God heals one issue or relationship may differ from the way He heals another. God is both creative and logical. Respect His sovereignty in every situation. Be flexible, open to change, and willing to try new things, even if they seem outside your comfort zone. God can do amazing things with a heart that is willing, submitted, forgiving, and obedient.

10. Be Hopeful. No matter how much murky water has passed under the bridge, God can cleanse and heal you. When you put your hope in Him, He will always provide a way to build a bridge of forgiveness so that, in faith, you can cross over to the other side. He is a God of second chances.

Different Bridges, Same Outcome

Different Bridges, Same Outcome · *7:02 minutes*

We drive over many different kinds of bridges during our marriage mission trips. Depending on the size of the gap spanned by the bridge, the time when the bridge was constructed, the geographical location and terrain, and the materials used, the bridges we cross appear different. But they all serve the same purpose: to get from one side of a chasm to the other.

The same holds true for your marriage. Because of the nature and consequences of different sins, it takes longer to build some bridges of forgiveness and faith than others—and you must figure in the assaults and accusations the Enemy will use to sideswipe you.

Some of the traumatic triggers you'll experience may bring to the surface such great pain that it takes a while to reveal the real root of the issue. Again, we emphasize that forgiveness and faith will result in the construction of a strong bridge that can hold the weight of *any* burden and help you cross over into new territories in your marriage.

Near the end of one of our mission trips, we experienced a small problem that led to a great divide. It's comical to think that it all started at the Grand Canyon.

Short on time, we'd slipped into a gift shop to grab a few post-cards for our supporters and some T-shirts for our family. Somehow in the transaction, we lost a credit card. It took several hours to realize the credit card was missing. That's when everything went downhill fast, and being exhausted didn't help. Losing the credit card set off one trigger after another, and eventually our conversation came to a halt. There was a Grand Canyon–sized gap in communication between us. Because we have an agreement about not raising our voices or speaking rudely to each other, we stopped our discussion and tabled it for a later time after we both cooled off.

It took us several weeks to sort through what transpired and figure out why the experience had instigated such a stalemate. During this time, we still talked to each other and demonstrated kindness; we just weren't ready to talk about what had happened. In the meantime, we individually went before God to help us forgive what we still didn't understand.

Gaining clarity about our conflict came slowly through spending time in God's Word and prayer—but it came. Forgiving each other *before* we were able to come to a full resolution and understanding of what had happened ensured that we continued to make progress on building the bridge over our divide.

The faith God required at that time was to fully entrust our frustration, anger, and other feelings into His hands while we sorted through the clutter. Then, when we were both ready, we were only continuing a bridge construction process that was already under way. Progress had not been halted due to harboring ill will or unforgiveness.

Our shortcomings and triggers can run deep, even spanning several generations. When you find yourselves standing at a chasm of Grand Canyon proportions, chances are you're dealing with much more than just the matter at hand. When we brought the lost credit card circumstance before God, He revealed the way it was rooted in old strongholds inherited from past generations. Clint's panic over the possibility of identity theft and fraudulent charges stirred up financial fears he'd lived with for decades. My flippant and carefree attitude about it was not in tune with what Clint was experiencing. As soon as he shared his feelings, I could understand why he reacted the way he did. At the time, I was angry at what I felt was an overreaction on his part. Clint explained that his grandmother had lost everything several times over during the Great Depression and the wars she'd lived through. His mother had also endured financial hardship after his father died, and Clint had suffered financial problems prior to our remarriage.

Although I couldn't relate to any of those experiences, I now understood where Clint was coming from. In addition, he realized I wasn't trying to act like what happened was no big deal when I suggested he just lighten up while I made a quick call to cancel the card.

Accurately assessing and sifting through conflict, no matter how painful or involved the process might be, ensures that the bridge you build through forgiveness and faith will do its job. When you intentionally and reverently allow God to work through the pain and mend the gaps in your marriage, He will safely carry you to the other side. Soon you'll discover that traumatic triggers happen less frequently, and when they do, you'll know exactly how to cross over them. In addition, you'll find that God is using them to enrich your marriage and deepen your dialogue—the topic of the next chapter.

Prayer to Build Bridges of Forgiveness and Faith

Father, we invite You to examine us. We confess our sins to You, repent of them, and receive Your forgiveness. Help us forgive ourselves and each other. Show us the ways You want us to change. Grant us the desire and courage to forgive one another for the ways we've been hurt with actions and words. We ask for Your wisdom to help us deal with the memories that trigger old wounds. When painful memories surface, help us recognize them and renounce the Enemy's attempt to divide us. If our circumstances generate responses and emotions based on past generations or our upbringings, clearly reveal these mysteries to us. Show us how to build bridges of forgiveness and faith over these painful places. Redeem the poor choices we've made in the past and use them for Your glory. In Jesus' name. Amen.

For a Marriage on the Mend

Identifying Related Issues

Harboring unforgiveness is often the source of other issues in your life. Look at the list below and place a check mark next to any of the symptoms you've experienced in the last six months. Is unforgiveness manifesting itself in any of the conditions listed? If so, ask God for the wisdom to deal with these things appropriately. Take some time during the coming week to write down the ways in which these related issues have surfaced. Be willing to seek professional help if necessary. Many times, when the cause is treated, the symptoms cease.

___ Depression	___ Anxiety/fear
___ Rage	___ Anger
___ Physical abuse	___ Chaos
___ Obsessive thoughts	___ Guilt
___ Weight gain/loss	___ Obsessive behaviors
___ Sleeplessness	___ Chemical abuse

Questions to Consider

1. Do you find it more difficult to extend forgiveness or ask your spouse for forgiveness? Why do you think this is?

2. What do you think the risks were in Nehemiah's conversation with King Artaxerxes in Nehemiah 2?

3. Describe a time when you asked someone for forgiveness. What was the person's response and how did it impact you?

4. Is there anyone from whom you need to ask forgiveness? What is holding you back from doing so?

5. What kinds of conversations are the most difficult for you to engage in with your spouse? Why do you think this is?

6. Look over the negative events you've listed on your marriage timeline. Are there any areas where you may still be harboring bitterness against your spouse for what occurred? If so, confess those things to God and your spouse. Seek forgiveness. Extend forgiveness.

Chapter 5

Deepening Your Discussions

One of the difficulties you'll encounter during the restoration process is the challenge of reestablishing healthy communication, or perhaps establishing it for the first time. In our case, there was a huge gap between the last time we'd spoken to each other, which was the day our divorce papers were notarized, and our next conversation more than a decade later. Our last few interactions as husband and wife had been extremely strained. I (Penny) became so angry that I threw my wedding ring across the room at Clint.

But because we had spent years focusing on our individual relationships with God before remarrying, we knew we could rely on Him to help us construct healthy communication.

It will take time for you to reestablish edifying lines of communication. Again, the key to healthy communication is maintaining a reconciled relationship with God and learning to rely on the Holy Spirit for help. Conversations with your spouse (which include speaking and listening) should always flow out of your conversations with God. If you're spending time with Him, then communicating with each other—no matter how difficult—will gain a more natural rhythm. You'll engage in discussions that please God and edify each other. Over time, the content of your dialogue will deepen as well.

We refer to this more challenging level of necessary dialogue as *courageous conversation*, a concept we teach in our seminars. The challenge courageous conversation poses for couples, especially those who have been through a crisis, is that most people avoid such discussions, fearing they will lead to more conflict. But we've discovered that the opposite is true. Intentionally engaging in courageous conversation actually alleviates conflict because there is already an underlying understanding between spouses. When you intentionally talk through challenging issues, you have the opportunity to understand each other's hot spots instead of being caught off-guard by them. Moreover, proactively engaging in courageous conversation means that neither spouse is left to flounder in reactive emotions when faced with sticky situations.

Deepening your dialogue means the two of you will have conversations that feel risky—because they *are* risky. But they are also vital to the restoration and overall health and growth of your relationship.

We were first introduced to the need for courageous conversation by our mentors, Dale and Colleen, who shepherded us during our first few years of remarriage. The honesty and forthrightness in their marriage inspired us to desire more authentic communication in ours.

It all began with a question: "Clint and Penny, how is your marriage affair-proof?" They wanted to know what plans we'd made to eliminate any possibility of either of us winding up in compromising situations. This level of dialogue was brand new for us.

Over the years, we've carefully listened as Dale, who is a pastor, and Colleen have shared more than thirty years of courageous conversations such as their own affair-proof plan. Early in their marriage they agreed upon certain nonnegotiable standards when it came to interacting with others. They weren't afraid to talk openly about staying out of questionable situations that might put either of them into a compromising scenario with a person of the opposite sex. They even spoke about these agreements with their close friends, like us, in order to proactively alleviate any misunderstandings down the road. We've been deeply impacted by the ways Dale and Colleen talk frankly and fearlessly about *every* aspect of their marriage.

Deepening Your Discussions, Part 1 · *5:05 minutes*

Jesus Tackled the Tough Topics

Courageous conversation between most spouses feels strange at first. That is why it's called *courageous*. The Bible is full of these types of conversations, and no one engaged in such dicey dialogue with more love, gentleness, and purpose than Jesus. Take, for example, His conversation with the woman at the well.

> The woman said to him, "Sir, give me this water so that I won't get thirsty and have to keep coming here to draw water."
> He told her, "Go, call your husband and come back."
> "I have no husband," she replied.
> Jesus said to her, "You are right when you say you have no husband. The fact is, you have had five husbands, and the man you now have is not your husband. What you have just said is quite true." (John 4:15–18)

Jesus' conversation with this woman was courageous in several ways. First, He was taking a double-sized risk. Jews and Samaritans did not associate with one another, and it was also against social practices for a man and woman to converse alone.

Second, Jesus tackled a very tough subject at the well. He knew this woman wasn't living in a right relationship with God and that the man she was living with wasn't her husband. Notice, however, that even though Jesus got to the heart of the matter, He did so with love, honesty, and truth. Jesus' willingness to engage in this exchange of dialogue dramatically impacted the woman's life and, for that matter, altered the entire course of human history. Following their conversation, the woman went into town and told others about Jesus (vv. 28–29). As a result of her testimony, many Samaritans believed that Jesus was the Savior of the world (vv. 39–42).

We had no affair-proof plan back when Dale and Colleen asked us that pivotal question, but we have one now. And it took several courageous conversations to get there. Since then, we've had many others. Courageous conversation is now a regular and integral part of our marriage.

Our man, Nehemiah, came face-to-face with the need to effectively and courageously communicate with people from all walks of life. As a layman, we can assume he wasn't highly trained in communication skills, especially in regard to royalty. However, God had divinely gifted this man and placed him in positions where quality communication skills were of the utmost importance.

Nehemiah's conversation with King Artaxerxes regarding his desire to leave his position of royal service and return to Jerusalem was definitely on the cutting edge. We can learn a great deal by carefully dissecting their conversation, extracting the essence of Nehemiah's approach and applying it to marriage. Elements of their conversation as recorded in Nehemiah 2 merit serious investigation, for they hold the power to transform communication with your spouse from idle chitchat, petty arguments, and major blowouts into meaningful discussions that will deepen the intimacy in your marriage.

In the month of Nisan in the twentieth year of King Artaxerxes, when wine was brought for him, I took the wine and gave it to the king. I had not been sad in his presence before, so the king asked me, "Why does your face look so sad when you are not ill? This can be nothing but sadness of heart."

I was very much afraid, but I said to the king, "May the king live forever! Why should my face not look sad when the city where my ancestors are buried lies in ruins, and its gates have been destroyed by fire?"

The king said to me, "What is it you want?" (Neh. 2:1–4)

As the king's cupbearer, Nehemiah had a hazardous job. It was his responsibility to taste everything before it was given to the king. If Artaxerxes wanted a cup of wine, Nehemiah sampled it first, and if he suffered no harm, then the king would partake. On this particular day, Nehemiah's already risky job led to a conversation that perched him on a razor's edge. Sadness was forbidden in the presence of the king, who with a mere gesture could order Nehemiah's execution.

Risk is the primary consideration of deeper discussions. Nehemiah's conversation with the king was a brave move. Again, the king had the power to imprison Nehemiah or end his life. Obviously, neither you nor your spouse possesses that kind of power. However, much of the heartache in a broken marriage comes from the words you've said—or should have said but didn't. Those are marriage killers.

We encourage you not to take the easy way out by giving in to the status quo. Regularly engaging in courageous conversation deprives the Enemy of opportunities to derail your marriage through misunderstanding. Let's continue exploring Nehemiah's conversation in order to discover the six key communication tools that are an integral part of cultivating healthy conversations.

Communication Tool 1: *Study Your Spouse*

As cupbearer, Nehemiah was often in the king's presence. He knew the king's likes and dislikes. He observed the ways the king operated and knew what made him tick. Nehemiah got to know the king, and we can safely assume that the king got to know Nehemiah as well. They must have had a fairly established relationship; otherwise, the king never would have noticed the uncharacteristic look of sadness on Nehemiah's face.

A couple of other principles can also be extrapolated from this passage. One is that you must have an established relationship with God as your king. Like Nehemiah, be in the King's presence often. Through His Word, prayer, and worship, continue to learn God's likes and dislikes as well as carefully observe the ways He works. Make an effort to study God.

The same holds true for your relationship with your mate. Spend time in careful observation. Get to know your spouse's likes and dislikes and establish a relationship of mutual trust. Effective communication grows out of studying and knowing each other. Safety in being vulnerable comes when you spend time together and intentionally work to rebuild trust. (More information on rebuilding trust will be discussed in chapter 6).

When we remarried, we were overwhelmed by the number of years and events we'd missed in each other's lives and the lives of our in-laws. We really didn't know each other. Weddings, graduations, birthdays, losses, and many other important life experiences had passed during our years apart. In order to get to know each other, we looked through photos and watched videos from the years we were divorced. We also shared journal entries and mementos from special events. The time spent sharing those things filled in some major missing pieces.

Whether or not your marriage crisis included separation or divorce, consider new ways you can deliberately spend time getting to know each other better. There are few things more comforting than being truly known by your spouse and investing your time and energy into increasing your knowledge of him or her. If you've been apart, think about ways to communicate the changes that occurred in your lives during that time. However, be sensitive to your spouse's feelings, reactions, and body language, because traumatic triggers can unexpectedly surface when discussing events from the past. Remember, the intent is getting to know each other better and expressing your love, not rehashing old problems.

Communication Tool 2:
Honestly Acknowledge Your Fear and Discomfort

The king's royal servants were expected to maintain composure at all times. But Nehemiah candidly confesses that he was "very much afraid" (Neh. 2:2). However, he didn't allow fear to paralyze him. Instead, his fear mobilized him to take a new step of faith: answering the king's question with confidence and honesty.

Paul and Diane (not their real names) had been married a few years when we met. By all outward appearances, they seemed to be progressing in their relationship. A short time later, however, they hit a point of crisis and came to us for help. Communication was at a standstill. When I had the opportunity to speak with Diane alone, she expressed her fears and struggles in discussing difficult subjects with Paul because of what happened to her as a child. Her primary caretaker, a very dominant authoritarian, was never approachable and always angry. This person was given to outbursts of anger, and Diane was now transferring her childhood experiences of fear and rejection onto her husband, expecting him to respond the same way her caretaker had. As a result, Diane avoided any measure of deep conversation with Paul and stayed at arm's length from him. Her upbringing automatically put her at a considerable distance away from her husband.

As we walked alongside this couple, we modeled a few basic skills which they adapted to fit their relationship. Paul soon realized that he could help Diane overcome her fears if he intentionally set aside time to talk, make eye contact, and take an interest in what she was saying. With practice, Paul's gentle demeanor comforted Diane and gave her the courage to speak up and share her feelings with more confidence. While there were other issues to work through, most of them stemmed from Diane's inability to express her feelings without fear of rejection. Since that time, Paul and Diane have steadily put the skills they've learned into practice, and both report they're much closer to each other.

Communication Tool 3:
Demonstrate Affirmation and Admiration

Nehemiah wasn't buttering up his boss when he exclaimed, "May the king live forever!" (Neh. 2:3). This was a common form of address to communicate respect to a king.

How do you commonly address your spouse? With respect? With love? Sometimes a word of affirmation, an appreciative tone of voice, or intentionally communicating kindness makes all the difference. If your mate thinks every discussion is going to be miserable or that he or she is going to be disrespected, devalued, or belittled, your spouse will feel reluctant to talk openly with you or listen to you.

In our own relationship, affirming each other as we tackle the tough topics has made a lot of difference in healing my (Clint's) reluctance to discuss my feelings and opinions. When we were married the first time, I shut down during difficult conversations because I felt like my opinions and feelings were going to be judged. I now understand that this stemmed from experiences in my past. Before I met Penny, I had a history of relationships that left me wounded when I reached out and risked vulnerability. Eventually

I gave up on sharing my thoughts and feelings. By the time Penny and I were married, I had made a subconscious decision to remain closed to conversations that required me to be vulnerable.

When we remarried, I told Penny about my struggles and expressed my desire to change. Just admitting the reluctance to share my true feelings and emotions helped Penny realize she could encourage me by being a good listener. Since then, she's affirmed me when I have new ideas or when I disclose my hopes and fears. In addition, during our discussions, Penny makes a point of complimenting the changes she sees in me regarding my openness and vulnerability. Her demeanor and kindness have made me want to share more of my heart with her.

Communication Tool 4:
Bathe Courageous Conversation in Prayer

Before Nehemiah told the king what was troubling him, he prayed (Neh. 2:4–5). We don't know exactly what he said to God in that moment, but we can assume it was probably something like, "Oh Lord, I'm nervous! Help me say what *You* want me to say!"

It's important that whenever you're going to engage in courageous conversation, you first spend time praying about it on your own. I think of Jesus as my first husband and Clint as my second. When there's something important I need to discuss with Clint, I take it to Jesus first, usually through writing in my journal. Sometimes I get only as far as bringing the matter before Him, and He lets me know that it's not the right time to bring it up to Clint or that I need to make a change in my own heart. Praying before a courageous conversation helps me share ideas and concerns with added love and gentleness. Prayer also makes me a more humble listener.

In addition to prayer, Clint and I never enter into these discussions without stating upfront that we'll be treading on holy ground.

It's our way of giving each other a heads-up. You may find it helpful to give your spouse some advance notice when the need for courageous conversation arises. That way your mate has time to prepare, and together you can choose an opportune time to talk. As a rule, courageous conversation should always be bathed in prayer before and after, and held in the privacy of your own home or a quiet place free from distractions.

Communication Tool 5:
Humbly Ask for What You Need

Nehemiah was specific with the king, letting him know exactly what he needed to be successful regarding his journey to Jerusalem.

> The king said to me, "What is it you want?"
> Then I prayed to the God of heaven, and I answered the king, "If it pleases the king and if your servant has found favor in his sight, let him send me to the city in Judah where my ancestors are buried so that I can rebuild it." (Neh. 2:4–5)

I used to find it extremely difficult to communicate my needs to Clint. I'd much rather have had him read my mind and instinctively know what I needed without my having to tell him. That kind of thinking created huge problems in our first marriage, and it has been a challenge for us this time around as well. Based on some experiences in my past, I'm reluctant to say what I need or want. Instead I allow my needs to dance around in my head, sometimes for weeks or months.

Over time, I finally learned to apply the principle of bringing my needs before Jesus as my first husband and Clint as my second. In prayer, I tell God what I need because I know He is more than capable of meeting all my needs. Then I let the Holy Spirit decide if my needs should be communicated to Clint and, if so, how I should go about it. During the years we've been remarried, I've had many opportunities to practice this process, and I learn a little more each time I take the risk.

Nehemiah's conversation with the king also illustrates two additional important principles for communicating your needs to your mate. First, you must be direct and concise. Nehemiah wanted to be released from his responsibilities as the king's cupbearer so he could go to Jerusalem, and that is exactly what he asked for. Nehemiah clearly expressed his need with confidence and respect. He wasn't demanding, but he knew how and when to cut right to the chase.

Wives, Nehemiah's approach is especially helpful in communicating with your husbands. Most men like their wives to spare the details and get to the point. I've often heard husbands say, "Just give me the bottom line."

I like detailed explanations and feel the need to share all the connections I see between the matters at hand. But Clint can get glossy-eyed when I give him too much information. It took me a while to figure this out and not let it frustrate me. With time and careful observation, I finally realized that Clint and I process information and details at different rates, and our brains are wired in such a way that the *kinds* of details we each want to know are very different. Clint likes information that involves numbers and patterns; he can remember anything that has to do with measurements, numbers, operations, or visual models. On the other hand, I like details regarding feelings, and I remember experiential things that are tied to emotion and depth. We finally realized these differences must be taken into account when we communicate with each other.

Like most couples, Clint and I fit the general stereotype that women tend to use more words and other means of communication—gestures, body language, facial expressions, and so forth—than men do. Clint says it jokingly but accurately in our seminars: "My wife needs to use about twenty thousand words a day. I've learned to let her get those words out. I only need to use about ten thousand. But I love my wife so much that I give her five thousand of my words so she can really have a good time."

Given the drastic differences between the sexes, there must be give-and-take in communication. It can't be all your way or your spouse's way. You must both learn to beat the statistics and stereotypes and come to a compromise.

That said, there is a time and place for more details, whether or not your spouse cares for them. Nehemiah must be commended for breaking male stereotypes. Even though he didn't go into a lot of detail with the king at first, he wasn't afraid to explain things further when he needed to.

> Then the king, with the queen sitting beside him, asked me, "How long will your journey take, and when will you get back?" It pleased the king to send me; so I set a time.
>
> I also said to him, "If it pleases the king, may I have letters to the governors of Trans-Euphrates, so that they will provide me safe-conduct until I arrive in Judah? And may I have a letter to Asaph, keeper of the royal park, so he will give me timber to make beams for the gates of the citadel by the temple and for the city wall and for the residence I will occupy?" (Neh. 2:6–8)

One commentary suggests that Nehemiah and the queen probably carried on many side conversations while the king was busy conducting the affairs of the kingdom. Perhaps the queen rubbed off on Nehemiah a bit. Whatever the case, he seemed to strike the perfect balance between not saying enough and saying too much. We can all stand to learn from his lead.

Communication Tool 6:
Prioritize Pleasing the King

Nehemiah used the phrase "if it pleases the king" twice in Nehemiah 2 (vv. 5, 7). He wanted to be sure all his requests were in alignment with what honored the king. Our conversations should also have as their goal God's pleasure and honor, not just ours. When the desire of your heart is to please God, harsh tones, negative statements, and outbursts of anger will be eliminated. That doesn't mean your dialogue will be dull or void of emotion, by any means. Nehemiah displayed emotion when he was sad of heart in the king's presence. Remember, he was so visibly upset that the king remarked on his emotional state.

Sometimes emotions get a bad rap, but deep discussions should include an appropriate expression of your emotions. *Appropriate* is the key word. God has emotions, and He carefully wired us with them as well. The Holy Spirit can temper emotions that aren't pleasing to God, such as outbursts of anger or rage.

I (Penny) grew up with quite a temper. At an early age I had a gruff vocabulary and learned to punch my way through elementary school as needed. It took a lot of hard work, but once I finally brought my anger before God, the Holy Spirit began sanding off my rough edges. So when people admit an anger problem to us, I can tell them confidently that if they really want to make a change, God will show them how.

Take Richard and Sharon for example. Very early in their marriage, they struggled with communication and conflict resolution. Their conversations stayed at a surface level, revolving around church responsibilities, raising their kids, and life on the farm. They argued constantly. A lack of emotional intimacy eventually took its toll. After seventeen years of marriage and four different counselors, Sharon decided their relationship was hopeless. They separated for sixteen months before things began to change.

"I wanted to obey God more than I wanted my own way," recalls Sharon. "God taught me that, without a doubt, He is trustworthy. He will never leave me and will always walk right beside me through everything—especially the hard times. Most of all, He taught me that when I give Him room to work, He will work miracles."

Besides deepening their individual relationships with God during their separation, Richard and Sharon told us that learning some basic communication tools through PAIRS, an organization that teaches relational skills, helped deepen their dialogue.[2]

"Using these skills gave us a safe environment to share our deepest selves—those parts of us that we'd never been able to share with each other. It gave us a way to walk through the past hurts and resolve our conflicts over them."

Richard and Sharon now teach these same communication tools to other couples.

"These tools were the catalyst for the miracle God did in rescuing our marriage," Richard shared. "In addition, we used these tools with our kids. Now they can also testify to God's faithfulness in their own lives during our separation and reconciliation. Even now, when problems arise, we pull out those same communication tools and use them. We're both sensitive to times when we feel ourselves heading for trouble, so we stop our conversation and say, 'We don't want to go there. We'd better use our tools.'"

In order to help you learn to engage in discussions that are pleasing to God, we've developed a list of ground rules that require a commitment from each of you.

 Deepening Your Discussions, Part 2 · *6:10 minutes*

Our Courageous Conversation Commitments

- We will pray before/after our courageous conversations.
- We will reveal our disappointments and inner fears.
- We will not reject each other.
- We will keep our hearts open and vulnerable.
- We will listen and not interrupt.
- We will make it safe to be honest.
- We will not use anything said as ammunition down the road.
- We will not attempt to manipulate, intimidate, or control each other.
- We will consider things from each other's viewpoint.
- We will not use harsh/rude tones or foul language.
- We will not place blame, make accusations, engage in fault finding, or throw things from the past in each other's face.
- We will hold each other accountable to God's desired outcomes.
- We will seek God's will each day by spending time alone with Him.
- We will not require the other person to meet our needs or expectations.
- We will apologize, seek forgiveness, and extend forgiveness to each other.
- We will view conflict as an opportunity for growth.

We encourage you to make these commitments, or modify our list to better fit your marriage. You'll find it helpful to review this list periodically.

It's tempting to sweep sensitive issues under the carpet because they're awkward to discuss. But whatever is kept in the dark can roadblock your relationship when you least expect it. Courageous conversation may be uncomfortable, but God can use it to create unity. Like Nehemiah, you'll discover that when you prayerfully and intentionally engage in courageous conversation, the final outcome is well worth the risk.

> Because the gracious hand of my God was on me, the king granted my requests. So I went to the governors of Trans-Euphrates and gave them the king's letters. The king had also sent army officers and cavalry with me. (Neh. 2:8–9)

Prayer to Deepen Your Discussions

Father, we want our conversations to please You and to be meaningful to our marriage. Please reveal the areas in which we need to communicate with more compassion, kindness, and honesty. Help us speak with humility, the way You did, Jesus. You never failed to communicate love or listen when people asked You questions and expressed their feelings. Teach us these skills. Use Your Holy Spirit to keep us in check when we fail to communicate in a healthy way and temper our emotions. Help us get to know each other better so we can learn how to effectively communicate, especially when it comes to handling tough topics. We understand there is a risk involved in having courageous conversations. We are willing to take that risk, but we can't do it without You. Grant us a more intimate relationship with each other through courageous and meaningful conversation. In Jesus' name we pray. Amen.

For a Marriage on the Mend

Making Connections

Write down some possible topics for courageous conversations that should occur in your marriage at this time or in the future.

Commit to praying about these conversations, and seek God's timing for engaging in them. Ask Him for wisdom before moving forward, but don't put off what you know must take place.

Questions to Consider

1. Describe the ways in which each of the following things contributes to courageous conversation: prayer, trust, honesty, body language, and cultural background.

2. How would you feel if you were in Nehemiah's shoes at this point in the rebuilding project (impatient, hopeful, focused, fearful, determined, frustrated, etc.)? Are there ways in which these feelings mirror your outlook on the restoration of your marriage? Be honest.

3. Discuss some of your thoughts and concerns about having courageous conversations. Can you think of any relationship or situation that caused conflict which could have been reduced or alleviated had a courageous conversation taken place beforehand?

4. Technological advances (such as the Internet, e-mail, cell phones, explicit movie channels, etc.) have created easy opportunities for people to get into compromising situations. How might a courageous conversation be helpful in avoiding these things?

5. Have you been adding positive and negative events to your marriage timeline? If not, take some time to do so, and discuss the ways proactive conversation can help to positively impact rough situations. Be sure to note times when you and your spouse viewed the same life event differently—that is, one of you viewed the event as positive and the other person viewed it as negative. Did your difference of opinion cause problems between you?

Chapter 6

Rebuilding on the Ruins of Your Past

A resilient relationship that can weather life's storms requires a deep level of mutual trust between spouses. Building mutual trust in a marriage isn't something that just happens naturally, and rebuilding trust after a crisis, separation, or divorce poses added challenges. It's a process that must be deliberately cultivated. Rebuilding trust requires prayer, practice, courageous conversation, and a willingness to work together, especially regarding the specific places where trust was betrayed.

As a marriage grows, there are levels of trust through which the relationship should progress. Because every marriage is unique, there is no rule book about what you'll discover at each level, how you get there, or exactly when deeper trust will take root. One thing can be said of all marriages, though: as you learn to trust God, He teaches you how to trust each other. This chapter focuses on the ways to rebuild trust in your marriage or, depending on your history, begin building a foundation of trust for the first time.

During our first marriage, we were stuck in a shallow level of trust and never progressed beyond it. Why? We didn't know how to *nurture* trust between us. We didn't realize that doing so would take time and diligent effort, and that as we intentionally practiced trusting God and each other, our trust would grow. The lack of trust in our first marriage was also due in part to our unwillingness to risk complete honesty. Neither of us wanted to come off as weak or needy, so we maintained a stiff upper lip no matter how hard things got. Translation: we were too proud to be vulnerable. A pattern of toughing it out kept repeating itself in both of our lives.

To complicate matters, we'd both experienced other relationships where trust was severely shattered and intimacy violated. As a result, we had each subconsciously determined never to let anyone get too close. During the two years we dated, we were mutually attracted to what we perceived as a tremendous amount of strength and self-discipline in each other's personality. But underneath our respective facades was raw pain which, for most of our lives, had gone unaddressed and been layered over with self-protection and pride. When we hit our first major conflict, all our unaddressed hurts rose up and broke through the veneer. Instead of getting help to deal with those hurts and losses, the pain overflowed into every aspect of our relationship and obscured what was really going on. It's highly likely that your own crisis, separation, or divorce has involved broken trust and losses that were never grieved.

During the years we were divorced, we both received some biblically based counseling. Seeking God for our individual restoration and devoting the time it took to heal was worth every penny spent. Neither of us realized how much pain we had stuffed down as a result of the severed trust in our lives, or how our hurtful experiences had affected our interactions as husband and wife. Unfortunately, the intimacy that marriage requires is often the perfect catalyst for unaddressed pain to surface. Like many couples, instead of honestly disclosing our wounds to each other, we covered over them and kept on going. But you can live like that for only so long. Eventually, something's got to give—either you or your marriage.

A word of caution before we proceed further. The experiences we share in this chapter from our own and others' relationships are meant to help you learn how to rebuild trust; however, the ways God restored trust in these marriages may differ from yours. In other words, the stories we share are not meant to be prescriptive. We won't spoon-feed you with a step-by-step list of exactly what you should do to deepen trust. Every marriage survival story is different. Rather, we share the stories here because we believe they're valuable to your journey, and they contain general principles that can apply to your circumstances. Please suspend making decisions about how you'll approach rebuilding trust until you've read the entire chapter and prayed fervently. It matters that much.

Hitting Rock Bottom

Four years after remarrying, we had the opportunity to visit Israel with a group from our church. Touring Jerusalem and taking in the sites was fascinating, but it was the time spent walking amongst the ruins of Beth Shean that impacted us beyond anything we'd expected. Located on the ancient trade routes between Mesopotamia and the Mediterranean Sea, Beth Shean was a large city that fell to the Philistines in the eleventh century B.C. Centuries later, Beth Shean became a flourishing city under the Byzantines until economic collapse and an earthquake in A.D. 749 reduced it to rubble.

"That's what our marriage looked like when we hit bottom," Clint whispered as we walked together, snapping photos at every turn. He was right. When our marriage came crashing down, it was nothing more than scattered rubble and debris. Any shallow measure of trust we'd developed during our brief first marriage was completely shattered when we separated and divorced.

While in Israel, our guide explained that archaeologists have been excavating the ruins at Beth Shean over a period of many years.

During our tour, we were fortunate to see the partial reconstruction of its ancient streets, columns, and walls. We realized the powerful analogy between the work of the archaeologists to rebuild the ancient city and the trust we needed to rebuild in our marriage.

Like trained archaeologists, you too can learn from your past in order to rebuild for your future. This chapter will put some new tools in your marriage tool belt.

Rediscovering the Past

The day we walked around Beth Shean, we were intrigued by the oddly shaped hills surrounding the site—hills with steep inclines and perfectly flat tops. Our guide explained that these hills were commonly referred to as *tels* (as in Tel Aviv). A tel is formed when ruined civilizations are leveled and new civilizations are built on top of the same site. Over time, the level of each new city rises; hence the tel's distinct shape. Civilizations dating from the Early Bronze Age to the Medieval Period had been discovered at Beth Shean, with each new civilization building on the preceding one. For various political, economic, and religious reasons, rebuilding a new civilization on top of a ruined one was a common practice for thousands of years.

We see evidence of this practice in the Bible. The book of Jeremiah records the following regarding the future restoration of Israel following their captivity:

> "I will restore you to health and heal your wounds," declares the LORD, "because you are called an outcast, Zion for whom no one cares."
>
> This is what the LORD says: "I will restore the fortunes of Jacob's tents and have compassion on his dwellings; the city will be rebuilt *on her ruins*, and the palace will stand in its proper place." (Jer. 30:17–18, emphasis added)

Retired archaeologist K. Kris Hirst speculates that civilizations built on the ruins of other civilizations to obtain a clear conscience.[3] They wanted to wipe the slate clean and start over, to do things better than they had been done before.

The same can be said for you. Some of your marriage ruins exist because trust was broken along the way, but the slate can be cleared and you can start over. Getting a fresh start begins when you acknowledge the painful experiences that have occurred and ask God to rebuild your relationship in those very same places. Although it isn't easy to revisit the past, God can be trusted with the process. He will never sever trust or take advantage of you. God is incapable of breaking trust because He is holy and perfect. Acknowledge that God is the only One who is fully trustworthy, and ask Him to show you how to nurture and build trust in the areas where trust was broken.

For example, because our marriage history included infidelity, we had a lot of work to do in that area. Outstanding resources are available today to help couples rebuild trust after infidelity, but back then we were unsure how to proceed. We didn't realize that others had successfully navigated the waters before us. Although our lack of knowledge and resources posed a challenge, we learned to consistently ask God for help.

In one of our most intimate experiences in the process of rebuilding trust, Penny shared something with me that she'd written many years before we reconnected. One of the assignments she completed in counseling was to write out her sexual history. What Penny wrote included some painful events from her childhood and adolescence as well as experiences later in life. She never imagined she'd ever be sharing these intimate secrets with me.

Before reading her sexual history to me, Penny explained that she had returned to these painful places where intimacy and trust were broken in order to truly heal. While she took full responsibility for her choices at the end of our first marriage, she had learned how other inappropriate sexual incidents had unified and surfaced, fueling her ability to walk out on me and never look back. In her eyes, I was just another man who had let her down.

Like an archaeologist, Penny was carefully exposing her past in order to learn from it and change her future. I'll never forget how I felt as she read what she'd written.

"I'm so sorry, Penny," I said, choking back the tears. "I had no idea."

Penny's willingness to expose her ruins made it safe to share mine. Using my journals from our years apart, I told Penny about the places in my past where intimacy had been violated, and I revealed the shame I'd unknowingly carried from those traumatic incidents. Disclosing my secrets helped Penny see that my John Wayne "suck it up, pilgrim" personality had been a form of self-protection.

Since then, our times of exposing past secrets have been some of our most intimate moments. These experiences have nurtured and deepened trust. By prayerfully excavating the ruins of our past, we've put together more of the pieces regarding why our first marriage didn't make it. This process allowed God to take those broken pieces and from them mold a new marriage we never dreamed possible.

Rebuilding Trust with Tenderness · *4:46 minutes*

Rebuilding Trust with Tenderness

Before excavating a site, an archaeologist thoroughly surveys the landscape in order to note specific points of interest. Important data is gathered, and decisions are made about how to approach the dig. The archaeologist also figures out which tools should be used in each area. Once the excavation begins, the archaeological team proceeds with great care, using fine tools and precise instruments in the most delicate areas. Because the site may contain rare and fragile treasures, trained archaeologists know it's wise to err on the side of caution when digging. In delicate places, a magnifying glass, small trowel, and fine brush are used to dust off years of dirt and grit.

The same holds true for the process of exposing the ruins of your past and rebuilding trust in those places. Some of the exercises we've encouraged you to complete, such as the inventory of your roadblocks, are like a survey of your marriage landscape. As you continue the restoration process in these delicate areas, it's essential to proceed with tenderness. Ask the Holy Spirit to help you blow the cakes of dirt and dust off places of past betrayal and expose what needs to be held up to the healing light of Christ. An important goal of this whole process is to understand what happened in the past and identify the tool that is needed to rebuild trust for each person.

Some archaeologists specialize in recovering evidence from battlefields and war zones in order to discover what truths the ruins have to reveal. Consider yourselves battlefield archaeologists who want to learn as much as possible from past conflicts in order to avoid recurrences. In the areas of your marriage where wounds are still raw and emotions fragile, demonstrate extra gentleness and care. Most importantly, don't use a backhoe! These places require the use of fine instruments—a skilled hand and a gentle heart.

Several months after I received Penny's letter of apology and we started pursuing reconciliation, we decided to meet face-to-face. We felt that spending some quality time together would help us know if remarrying each other was God's will. Because we wanted our time together to be free from distractions, we decided to meet on neutral territory between my home in Florida and Penny's home in California. Beforehand, we committed to handling our physical contact appropriately: maintaining healthy boundaries and having separate hotel rooms. We also asked a group of mature believers to pray for us and hold us accountable.

After much anticipation, Penny and I set eyes on each other in the terminal of the Denver International Airport for the first time in over a decade. Our reunion was something we'll never forget. Our first embrace felt like slipping a familiar hand into a tailored glove—a perfect, seamless fit.

By far, one of the most important things we did that weekend was to get honest with each other about the specific ways in which trust had been broken and expose the guilt and shame we'd carried. This was extremely delicate work, to say the least.

Saturday morning, we packed a picnic lunch and drove to a park in downtown Denver. In a secluded spot, we spread out a blanket and unpacked the journals we'd kept during our years apart. For several hours, we took turns reading old entries, talking about the past, and weeping together. Because we never intended to share those journals with anyone but God, the thoughts we'd expressed were raw and honest. That day, we asked each other many questions and disclosed things we'd never shared with anyone. Penny answered all the questions I had about the affair that ended our marriage as well as many other things that had transpired between us. Penny asked me several poignant questions as well.

At one point in our conversation, I remember looking at Penny and asking, "Didn't you know you were the love of my life?"

"No, Clint," she responded. "I really didn't."

Penny's answer gave me the opportunity to apologize for never communicating the depth of my love when we were married, and it helped me understand how she felt back then. Because we'd bathed our meeting in prayer and had other people praying, our courageous conversations that weekend, although difficult, were full of tenderness and compassion.

Since then, we've come to understand that we should never be afraid of engaging in those kinds of discussions, especially about intimacy and trust. They are well worth the discomfort.

A powerful way to jumpstart this kind of discussion and rebuild trust is to extend the marriage timeline we suggested you create at the end of chapter 1. Using a different colored pen, each of you should extend the timeline back into your respective childhoods to identify places where trust and intimacy were violated or betrayed. Pay specific attention to life events such as divorce, physical or emotional abuse, tragedy, molestation, or the death of loved ones. Tracing these specific issues back over your lives will help you engage in deep discussions. It will also help identify the ways those violations and circumstances contributed to the crisis in your marriage, and it may provide explanations—not justifications—for your attitudes and behaviors.

As you discuss the past, it's imperative that you give your spouse the gift of your discretion. The intimate things disclosed in private shouldn't be discussed with others without your spouse's permission. In general, unless someone's life is in danger, it's inappropriate to share something your spouse has asked you to keep confidential. Use wise judgment. Nothing breaks trust faster than a breech in confidentiality between spouses.

What the Evidence Tells Us

Another part of an archaeologist's job is to accurately interpret evidence from an excavation. All unearthed artifacts are carefully studied, catalogued, classified, and analyzed in an effort to discover the answer to one important question: What do these treasures tell us?

In revisiting our pasts, Penny and I were doing the very same thing. Instead of looking at our history with shame and confusion, as we had for decades, we finally viewed the "artifacts" we unearthed as rare treasures—which is exactly how God saw them all along.

That weekend in Denver, we put God in charge of reconstructing the past in order to help us create a more meaningful future. Through this process, we were able to examine the ancient relics from our lives, gain from them a greater understanding about past behaviors, and figure out why our first marriage failed so miserably so quickly. All the mysteries we'd wondered about for years finally made sense.

Other couples have made the same discovery. We met Scott and Cathy (you heard from them in chapter 2) after a workshop we were teaching for pastors and ministry leaders. Their outright honesty in unpacking their saved-marriage story was proof that they had done the hard work of dusting off all the drama from their crisis and uncovering the real root of their division. After getting to know them, we asked about the excavation process they had gone through and the ways it had positively impacted their marriage.

"It wasn't easy," said Scott. "But I really felt that in order to truly heal, we both had to be willing to pray through all the deep darkness and bring everything into the light."

Cathy continued their story.

"Opening the lines of communication about our pasts meant we had to be vulnerable with each other. But as a result, what we have together now exceeds what I ever imagined our marriage could be. People talk about wanting a fairy-tale marriage. What Scott and I have is far better."

Talking About Trust · *5:22 minutes*

Talking About Trust

As with any grand-scale excavation, rebuilding trust is a process that occurs over a period of months and years. It takes a commitment to have intentional, meaningful, and courageous conversation and to develop good listening skills. We find it helpful to regularly schedule uninterrupted times to talk about rebuilding trust in specific areas. During these conversations, Penny asks me questions such as, "How are you feeling about my friendships with others? Do you have any concerns you'd like to share? Is there anything I'm doing that is causing you not to trust me?"

These questions encourage me to share my concerns or feelings regarding my trust in Penny. During these conversations, we both know in advance that we're entering into intentional discussions about trust instead of just reacting to awkward circumstances or catching each other off-guard.

Asking important questions about trust goes both ways. I don't want Penny to live with a shadow of mistrust hanging over her head whenever I'm not around, and she doesn't either. To alleviate this, I ask her questions such as, "Do you feel like you have the freedom to spend time with others? Do you sense that I'm trying to control you in any way?" My questions provide Penny with the opportunity to share her feelings and pinpoint specific concerns about trust. As we regularly engage in this back-and-forth process, greater trust is forming.

A word to those of you who walked out on your marriage or feel the brunt of the blame: Although our first marriage ended when Penny left, I never wanted her to feel like she was the one who bore all the responsibility. My closed demeanor and tough-guy attitude also contributed to our breakdown. Indicating through my behavior and words that Penny should just suck it up when it came to our problems definitely didn't help keep the lines of communication open. My lack of emotion and compassion made it difficult for her to tell me anything. So in our remarriage, I had to work just as hard to rebuild trust with Penny as she did with me—and the same holds true for you. No matter who did what in your marriage, rebuilding trust is a two-way street.

Regularly setting aside time to talk about trust also involves learning ways to strengthen each other's trust. People's needs differ. What I need Penny to do to build my trust is different from what she needs me to do to nurture hers. For example, Penny leaves a note or message when she goes somewhere. That way, when I come home to an empty house, I know why it is empty and where she is. Each time Penny does that, she rebuilds my trust in her.

I once told Penny I was concerned about our getting so busy that we wouldn't have time for each other. This was a problem in our first marriage, and our lack of meaningful interaction made it easier for the gap between us to widen and someone else to enter in. When we remarried, I was concerned that, if we weren't careful, the same thing could happen. Heading off in too many different directions was (and still is) a major red flag for me.

While Penny may not share this concern to the same degree, she respects my feelings and works to build trust in this area. She makes it a priority to keep ample margin and down time in our schedules. There are busy seasons for every family, but for the most part, we avoid getting overcommitted. By understanding and respecting what I need in this area, Penny demonstrates her trustworthiness to me in meaningful ways.

For Penny, trust was (and still is) rebuilt in our marriage when she feels the freedom to honestly disclose her greatest fears and worries without reservation. She isn't accustomed to letting anyone into those vulnerable places. But now I know that about her. Therefore I make a point of listening to her concerns with compassion. Because I know she's hesitant to express her feelings and needs, I've learned to ask specific questions such as, "What do you need from me right now? Do you want my help, or do you want me to just listen?"

Like most men, my tendency is to swoop in and try to solve my wife's problems. But most often, Penny doesn't want me to fix anything. She wants me to listen and to know her. My supportive reactions cause Penny to trust me with her feelings to a greater degree. On the other hand, if I withdraw my support or am not interested in her concerns, she feels distant, and rather than growing, trust between us becomes stagnant.

Our conversations also give us the opportunity to comment on the ways we notice each other intentionally demonstrating trust-inspiring actions and attitudes. Making a point to acknowledge and compliment each other's efforts will deepen the intimacy in your own marriage and draw you closer together.

Joe and Michelle were separated multiple times before they finally began the process of rebuilding trust. "Rebuilding trust has been a daily process ever since we reconciled," Joe shared during one of our many conversations. "We both realize there are some deep wounds the Enemy can raise up at any moment, and we don't ever take our reconciliation for granted. When old triggers from past pain or conflict creep into our relationship, we wait for the panicky thoughts to subside. Then we both put truth into our situation."

As founders of Marriage 911 God's Way (marriage911godsway .com) and authors of the book *Yes, Your Marriage Can Be Saved*, Joe and Michelle are honest about the ongoing process of rebuilding trust. "One thing that still triggers old stuff for me," Michelle admitted, "is when I take longer to get home than I expected and Joe calls to ask me what's taking so long. I have to be really careful that I don't assume he is mistrusting me but simply wants to know when I'll be home."

For Joe, an old button gets pushed when he starts to feel left out of the loop in planning. "I have to remind myself that it's my responsibility to speak up and ask Michelle to update the calendar rather than assuming she's leaving me out of something because she doesn't want me there."

Take the initiative to learn the specific areas in which your spouse struggles to trust you and also to feel trusted by you. This will take ongoing courageous conversations. Mark the red flag areas that come up for your spouse and discuss the ways you can respect those concerns. Remember, you may not share the same feelings or understand why they are important to your mate, but you can ask God to show you ways to demonstrate respect for what your spouse needs.

Rebuilding Trust with Your Children

We've waited till now to begin talking about the children who may be involved in your restoration.

The stress children internalize from what occurs between their parents or stepparents often manifests in the classroom and the playground. For example, students who are caught in the middle of marital turmoil often have difficulty focusing on their classwork, and their progress in school wanes as a result. Inappropriate behavior, missing homework, and poor physical health are just a few of the external signs that there may be problems at home.

Adult children obviously exhibit different signs than younger children do. What matters is for you to realize that regardless of their ages at the time of your crisis, separation, or divorce, their trust in you has been dramatically impacted. You must be willing to rise up, shelter them from further harm, and intentionally rebuild the trust of each child involved.

Couples often get so caught up in their crisis that they pay little attention to its tremendous effect on their kids. Security and safety are some of the core needs of children, and their parents' marriage crisis threatens those needs in significant ways. Your children will need a great deal of reassurance as your family is being restored. They must have a stable environment with set routines and expectations to combat and level out the chaos they've experienced.

Marriage problems stir up great uncertainty that children often absorb. Some children even feel responsible for the problems between their parents. When my parents announced their decision to divorce, somehow I (Penny) incorrectly assumed that I was a significant part of the problem. When they separated, the three younger children went to live with my mom and the three older children stayed with my dad. Our whole world was torn in two, and I unwittingly assumed the responsibility for fixing it. Many years later, I realized each one of us coped (and is still coping) with our parents' divorce in different ways according to our personalities, perceptions, and ages at the time.

Be intentional about including your children in the process of restoration. Your overall goal is to protect your family unit and provide for the immediate emotional, physical, and spiritual needs of each child.

Nehemiah recognized the importance of protecting the institution of the family during the restoration of Jerusalem:

> Meanwhile, the people in Judah said, "The strength of the laborers is giving out, and there is so much rubble that we cannot rebuild the wall."
>
> Also our enemies said, "Before they know it or see us, we will be right there among them and will kill them and put an end to the work."
>
> Then the Jews who lived near them came and told us ten times over, "Wherever you turn, they will attack us."
>
> Therefore I stationed some of the people behind the lowest points of the wall at the exposed places, posting them by families, with their swords, spears and bows. (Neh. 4:10–13)

Nehemiah recognized that if a builder were working on a section of the wall that was located far from his home, he wouldn't be able to protect his family. So he stationed workers by family groups and armed them with weapons to combat enemy attacks.

It's critical for you to regularly call your children together and arm them with strategies to deal with the struggles they've encountered as a result of your crisis. Don't ever be too proud to seek professional assistance when needed.

Trusting that Mom and Dad really are going to stay together is a hurdle your kids will need help getting over. Because the core of our entire existence is based upon the family unit, Satan wants nothing more than to tear families apart through betrayal and broken trust. Not only are you in a fight to restore your marriage, but you are also in a fight for your family.

> After I looked things over, I stood up and said to the nobles, the officials and the rest of the people, "Don't be afraid of them. Remember the Lord, who is great and awesome, and fight for your families, your sons and your daughters, your wives and your homes."
>
> When our enemies heard that we were aware of their plot and that God had frustrated it, we all returned to the wall, each to our own work. (Neh. 4:14–15)

Part of Nehemiah's strategy for the welfare and protection of the family unit was to help them "remember the Lord." This was Nehemiah's rallying cry in the midst of repeated attacks, because he knew that remembering what God had done in the past would dispel their present fears.

"Remember the Lord" should be the rallying cry of your family as well. The most effective way to help your family remember Him is to regularly gather for prayer and intentional conversation about how things are going. Specifically pray with your children to rebuild trust and unity as a family. Consider having a weekly family meeting specifically to discuss any concerns about the healing process. In addition, have your family memorize a Scripture verse each week. Some families find it helpful to keep a journal that serves as a record of their meetings. This journal can also contain prayer requests and answers to prayer, which can be an important way of reminding you of all that God has done and is doing.

An unfortunate consequence of marital turmoil is that children are sometimes exposed to much more than they should be. In the midst of heated arguments or attempts to retaliate, spouses often disclose things to their children that should never be revealed. Sometimes young children discover a parent's specific violations, such as infidelity or addiction, on their own or by overhearing adult conversations. Whatever the case, the trust and security a child had in one or both parents is shaken to the core.

If trust has been violated in that way, you have some added work to do. That work begins with prayer. Ask God what each child needs individually in order to regain trust in you. Rebuilding trust takes a great deal of time for children, depending on their ages, personalities, the history of your relationship, and the nature of what transpired. If you were separated from your kids, they will feel a sense of abandonment. They may even worry that each time an argument occurs, you'll separate again. Give your kids a safe place to discuss their fears, and be certain to address their concerns on a regular basis. Reassure your children that although Mom and Dad still have differences, you're both committed to making your marriage work and keeping the family together.

As with any other relationship where trust has been broken, nothing starts the healing process more effectively than asking for forgiveness and apologizing for the mistakes you've made. Don't miss out on any opportunity to model forgiveness and reconciliation with your kids. There are few things more powerful than having a humble parent kneel at their child's bedside, apologize, and ask for their forgiveness.

Treasuring Your Shared Past, Anticipating Your Shared Future

Although you can probably make a list of painful memories in your marriage that stretches for miles, you can rebuild trust by focusing on the memorable celebrations and favorite family events that are a part of your marriage history. For us, an important part of moving forward was to go back and revisit special places from our early years together and reclaim what the Enemy had stolen. We made a point of treasuring our shared past and focusing on the good things we remembered. For example, we revisited the marina where we were engaged in 1989. We had a great time talking about what happened that night and about our lofty ideals and unrealistic expectations. Looking through old photographs and videos was another way we treasured our history.

In addition to revisiting fond memories, we set a course to make new ones. Two years after we remarried, our church announced they were assisting in a makeover for a small church in a nearby city. Being a part of that project gave us the chance to serve alongside each other in a new way. We made many friends during the project, and the memory of our experience remains a highlight from the early years of our remarriage. Engaging in a family service project is one way to rebuild relationships. Serving others also helps take the focus off your circumstances and broadens your perspective.

Despite your best efforts, it's perfectly normal to experience occasional trust setbacks. But if you're both seeking God daily and being intentional about rebuilding trust, your relationship will grow and deepen. Exposing the ruins of betrayed trust to the light of Christ is critical for the health and restoration of your marriage. The same holds true for any trust setbacks that occur. Honestly acknowledge and confess your mistakes to God.

Always focus on *fact*-finding, not *fault*-finding. Like the archaeologist who gathers evidence to reconstruct events and make sense of them, you must keep the goals of learning from your mistakes and rebuilding trust at the forefront of your intentions. It is *never* appropriate to revisit the sins of the past in order to inflict pain. Nothing will set your marriage back more quickly than engaging in such unhealthy behavior. Instead, allow God to examine and restore broken trust from the past to positively impact your future.

Prayer to Rebuild Trust

Father, we desire to trust each other in a manner that communicates our love for You. In the past, we violated trust, and there were times when we didn't trust You. Forgive us, and heal the wounds of broken trust. Help us rebuild on the ruins of our past. Show us how to trust each other and nurture trust. Help us see opportunities to demonstrate trust as well as to be vulnerable without the fear of rejection. Teach us how to encourage trust in each other. Show us how to rebuild our children's trust in us and how to bring a sense of security to our family. Despite what has occurred, help us teach our children more about who You are. May they learn to trust You with their lives. Protect their vulnerabilities, and help us provide for their inner healing as well as their physical, emotional, social, and spiritual needs. May our trust in You create greater intimacy in our marriage and strength in our family. In Jesus' name. Amen.

For a Marriage on the Mend

Making Connections

Set aside uninterrupted time to discuss specific things you can do for your spouse to nurture trust. Make note of your similarities and differences. Consider creating a list of some key questions that you can ask each other when you need to have trust-building talks.

Questions to Consider

1. Skim back over Nehemiah 3. What did you notice about the manner in which Nehemiah proceeded with the rebuilding of Jerusalem's gates? How might this relate to restoring your marriage?

2. In which area of your life do you find it hardest to trust God? How does God nurture trust with you?

3. Do you consider yourself a trustworthy person? Give an example of a time when you were trustworthy in a difficult situation.

4. Consult the trust-building ideas presented in this chapter. What are some specific steps you will take this week to nurture more trust in your marriage?

5. Take out your marriage timeline, add some blank paper to the right side of it, and extend the horizontal line. This will represent the future of your marriage and the clean slate you've been given by God. What hopes do you have regarding the future of your relationship?

Chapter 7

Aligning Your Standards

Have you ever driven a vehicle that wasn't properly aligned? It veered to one side or the other, and you needed a firm grip on the wheel to drive it safely, right? In order for a car to travel straight down the road, the front end must be properly aligned and the tires balanced. The same can be said for your relationship. If your marriage isn't in proper alignment with the standards from God's Word, all it takes are a few bumps in the road to veer off course. In contrast, husbands and wives who make a deliberate, daily attempt to align their marriage with God's standards will develop a more resilient relationship.

When Clint and I were married the first time, we were both Christians. We attended church regularly and served God in many different ways. We thought that was enough to make for a strong marriage. But we were wrong. When challenges arose between us, we didn't know what to do because we hadn't spent time rooting our marriage in God's Word. To complicate matters, we were too proud and embarrassed to tell anyone our marriage was on shaky ground. When our pastor finally found out, I already had one foot out the door. Not until we were remarried did we come to understand that our marriage needed to be in complete alignment with the principles in the Bible.

What's Your Standard?

For the purposes of this book, let's define the word *standard* as "a criterion on which your marriage is based." Think of standards as the consensual focal points of your relationship. In chapter 11, we'll discuss the ways your marriage standards become the bar by which progress is measured. For now, let's establish the standards for a Christ-based marriage and the ways in which they should play out.

Subconsciously, everyone brings his or her own standards into a marriage. These standards are based on a variety of factors such as childhood upbringing, role models, past experiences, values, attitudes, culture, media, and beliefs. Chances are, neither you nor your spouse was aware of the standards you brought into your marriage or where they originated. For example, where did you derive your concepts about the division of roles and responsibilities in your household? What about the way conflict should be handled, or your spending and saving habits, or your ideas about parenting? Consider the marriages surrounding you when you were growing up. Did any of them furnish role models that impacted your views on marriage?

Many conflicts that divide a marriage arise from the different standards each spouse brought into the relationship. When these differences manifest in practical, daily life, they can create conflict.

I (Penny) grew up in a large Italian family with six children. When there was a conflict or crisis, everyone knew about it, even my extended family, and each person had an opinion to contribute. Arguments were loud occasions. Body language was demonstrative, emotions were dramatic, and explanations were exaggerated. The issue at hand was discussed with gusto until a resolution was reached. Conflict was a long and involved process. So naturally, my approach to dealing with conflict closely mirrored that model.

Clint, on the other hand, was raised with a drastically different model for conflict resolution. His family is of German descent. His only sibling was his younger sister and his parents were very reserved. Any problem was settled quickly and quietly and, more often than not, behind closed doors. What little discussion may have been required was void of high emotion.

Given our two drastically different families of origin, can you imagine what happened the first time Clint and I had a disagreement?

Many couples never realize how likely they are to experience a *cultural clash* when they marry. Your ethnicity greatly influences the standards you bring into marriage. The differences may be overt, such as skin color or language, or they may be more subtle, such as communication styles or family traditions. Whatever the case, cultural differences can be the source of intense conflict and can quickly zap your unity if they are not brought into submission under God.

Veering off Course

During our first marriage, I felt confused by Clint's reluctance to discuss problems. The more I persisted in wanting to talk through our differences, the more he shut down. As a result, my emotions grew steamy, which only made matters worse.

The night of our first major argument, we went to bed without having resolved the conflict. I cried myself to sleep, feeling disillusioned and misunderstood. The next morning, it seemed like there were miles between us in bed instead of just inches. Figuring I'd given Clint enough time to think, I brought the matter up again before the first cup of coffee was poured.

"So what are we going to do about this?" I asked, hoping to come to some kind of compromise.

Clint said nothing. Instead, he walked into the kitchen and made breakfast. As I had done the night before, I started filling up every molecule of air space with my opinions and emotions, determined to find the resolution that seemed to elude us. It never came. Conflicts after that only widened the existing gap between us. During our brief first marriage, every conflict we had got snagged in that same cycle.

Looking back, neither of us can remember the exact sources of our discontent. What we remember is the drastically different manners in which we approached conflict resolution, stemming from our respective upbringings. Herein is the problem most couples face. The manner of dealing with conflict for one spouse—that person's standard for conflict resolution—is not the same as that of the other.

Shortly after we remarried, we realized that aligning our standards for conflict resolution with biblical principles would create a well-rounded, resilient, and harmonious relationship, one that honored God even in the midst of conflict.

Nehemiah spoke of something similar when he set out to reform the Israelites and rebuild their community.

> "Remember the instruction you gave your servant Moses, saying, 'If you are unfaithful, I will scatter you among the nations, but if you return to me and obey my commands, then even if your exiled people are at the farthest horizon, I will gather them from there and bring them to the place I have chosen as a dwelling for my Name.'" (Neh. 1:8–9)

Being dispersed and exiled was a consequence of the people's not having their lives and relationships in alignment with the laws and commands that God had set down for them through Moses. Their disobedience resulted in broken relationships. Of utmost importance was their fractured covenant with God. And not living in alignment with His standards directly impacted their relationships with each other. In Nehemiah 5, we see another example of what happens when our interactions with God and one another are not in alignment with God's standards:

Now the men and their wives raised a great outcry against their fellow Jews. Some were saying, "We and our sons and daughters are numerous; in order for us to eat and stay alive, we must get grain."

Others were saying, "We are mortgaging our fields, our vineyards and our homes to get grain during the famine."

Still others were saying, "We have had to borrow money to pay the king's tax on our fields and vineyards. Although we are of the same flesh and blood as our fellow Jews and though our children are as good as theirs, yet we have to subject our sons and daughters to slavery. Some of our daughters have already been enslaved, but we are powerless, because our fields and our vineyards belong to others." (Neh. 5:1–5)

Nehemiah had his hands full. Food was scarce and taxes were high. The Jews were so engaged in rebuilding the city that they weren't completing the tasks necessary to maintain their own households. As a result, many people were forced to mortgage property to those who were in the business of lending. For a while, borrowing from their brethren didn't seem problematic. However, once the initial euphoria of the task at hand wore off, conflict arose that threatened to put a screeching halt to the rebuilding. By the time Nehemiah became aware of the problem, the disagreement had gotten way out of hand.

This time the opposition wasn't coming at Nehemiah from an outside source but from within the community he was attempting to help. Imagine what it must have been like to be right in the middle of this monumental project only to have a major outbreak of frustration, fear, and dissension amongst your co-laborers. Make no mistake: Satan was determined to do whatever he could to interrupt the rebuilding process by splintering relationships. The same holds true for our marriages today. The Enemy longs for our interactions and relationships to get out of alignment with God's Word and His ways. It doesn't take much to cause a great divide.

We can learn a valuable lesson from the way Nehemiah led God's people back into alignment with His laws. Look at his response to their conflict.

> When I heard their outcry and these charges, I was very angry. I pondered them in my mind and then accused the nobles and officials. I told them, "You are charging your own people interest!" So I called together a large meeting to deal with them and said: "As far as possible, we have bought back our fellow Jews who were sold to the Gentiles. Now you are selling your own people, only for them to be sold back to us!" They kept quiet, because they could find nothing to say.
>
> So I continued, "What you are doing is not right. Shouldn't you walk in the fear of our God to avoid the reproach of our Gentile enemies? I and my brothers and my men are also lending the people money and grain. But let us stop charging interest! Give back to them immediately their fields, vineyards, olive groves and houses, and also the interest you are charging them—one percent of the money, grain, new wine and olive oil." (Neh. 5:6–11)

Nehemiah knew God required something contrary to the ways His people were treating each other, and he wasn't afraid to call them on it. He brought the Jews into account by reminding them of God's expectations and standards for relationships. Look at the way the people responded to Nehemiah's realignment of their behavior: "'We will give it back,' they said. 'And we will not demand anything more from them. We will do as you say'" (Neh. 5:12).

Coming into Alignment

In order for God to restore your marriage, it is imperative that you take an honest look at the standards you subconsciously brought into your marriage, and that you agree to do the work necessary to base your relationship on God's standards—on the promises and principles found in His Word.

Begin by learning what God's standards are; then make a conscious effort to integrate them into your marriage. As discussed in chapter 3, healing happens naturally when you spend consistent time in God's Word. He makes the transformation and blending of your differences possible through the Holy Spirit, working in cooperation with His Word. Once those changes begin, God's standards need to be applied to your relationships and circumstances through obedience and faith.

The following example contains two standards that Clint and I have agreed on. Notice that each standard is matched with a verse or passage of Scripture. That way we're certain our standards are aligned with those in the Bible.

Standard 1: We will forgive one another's past mistakes and present faults. Nothing from the past will be thrown in each other's faces. "Therefore, as God's chosen people, holy and dearly loved, clothe yourselves with compassion, kindness, humility, gentleness and patience. Bear with each other and forgive one another if any of you has a grievance against someone. Forgive as the Lord forgave you" (Col. 3:12–13).

Standard 2: We commit to never speak rudely, harshly, or disrespectfully to each another in public or in private. "Do not let any unwholesome talk come out of your mouths, but only what is helpful for building others up according to their needs, that it may benefit those who listen" (Eph. 4:29).

Aligning Your Standards · 5:09 minutes

Developing our marriage standards didn't happen overnight but over a period of many months. The process started with prayer. When we asked God to reveal the places in our marriage that were out of alignment with His Word, it didn't take long for a list to begin forming. We also looked honestly at the areas of our greatest disagreements. For example, given the differences in the ways our families of origin dealt with conflict, we knew we needed a standard to help us handle our disagreements appropriately: not my way, not Clint's way, but God's way.

During our time in the Word, we took note of any verses that exemplified the ways we wanted to interact with each other. Then we developed written standards that reflected each of those qualities. Not only did this process ensure that our marriage was based on God's standards, but as a bonus, it also helped us spend time in the Word together.

We talked with other Christian couples who had stable and godly marriages. We observed their interactions and discussed aspects of their relationships that we desired for our own. We also noted couples who interacted in a manner we didn't like; discussing and learning from their negative behavior was also important.

Paul and Linda's marriage was one we grew to admire, although we had no idea of their backstory until we got to know them. As it turned out, Paul and Linda had divorced one month after their eighteenth anniversary.

"I never thought we should have divorced," shared Paul. "Soon after we went our separate ways, I was filled with the hope that one day Linda and I would remarry. We were both raised in Christian homes. What we'd done was against God's will, and deep down we both knew it. Our divorce lasted sixteen months. Then it was as if God grabbed our attention and let us both know that we had to take responsibility for what we had done."

Linda continued. "God showed us how we got into trouble because we hadn't put Christ at the center of our marriage. When I asked God to restore us, He gave me more of a husband and marriage than I could have ever imagined. I couldn't have asked for the regaining of trust, healing, forgiveness, and restoration He provided.

"It was the Bible that brought us back to our roots. Together, we vowed to keep Christ in the center of our lives and marriage the second time around. Our hunger for Christ began to increase, and we desperately wanted a marriage that would be grounded in the Word.

"There are several ways Paul and I have kept our marriage fixed on God's Word during the years we've been remarried. After breakfast, we lay out all our thanksgivings and petitions and then put on the whole armor of God. When we sit down to work on projects or have major decisions to make, we pray beforehand, which keeps the standards in His Word at the center. Before retiring at night, we have a devotional time which also keeps God at the forefront of our relationship. This encourages us to discuss the things we normally wouldn't have time to talk about during the day."

Paul continued where Linda left off. "The three main biblical standards we have consist of keeping pure in heart, spending time in the Word, and praying together. There are also several verses at the core of who we are as husband and wife. Ephesians 5:25 says, 'Husbands, love your wives, just as Christ loved the church and gave himself up for her.' We see this as the ultimate sacrificial love that says, 'I'll die for you.' This standard brings real meaning to the unconditional love we share.

"These standards weren't part of us in our first marriage, but they're the foundation of our reconciliation. God is amazing, and

He has done incredible things in our lives, for which we're very thankful."

Like Paul and Linda, we've created some marriage standards you may find useful. We share these in order to give you a better idea of how God's Word can play out in your marriage every day.

Sample Marriage Standards

- We will love one another and joyfully fulfill our marriage vows of lifetime fidelity.
- We will be as polite to one another as we are to our friends and colleagues.
- We will abstain from the use of any form of pornography or the viewing of degrading movies, television programs, Web sites, or other inappropriate media.
- We will thank God for our meals before we partake of them.
- We will regularly attend worship services and serve together.
- We will work out our conflicts and problems in truth and honesty, without unhealthy interference or excess drama from relatives or friends.
- We will give from a generous heart, tithing at least ten percent of our income, and we will work out a shared partnership for all purchases, expenses, and other financial matters.
- We will humbly dedicate our lives, family, home, and material possessions to Christ and practice His teachings by being loyal, loving, and generous in all circumstances.
- We will cultivate a healthy sense of humor and engage in common activities together.

Some couples we've met over the years have written down their standards, framed them, and hung them up in their homes. Others have expanded their standards to include some for parenting and extended family relationships. Call your children together so everyone can give input as to how the family should function based on God's Word. We encourage families to work together to write down their standards and corresponding Bible verses on large sheets of butcher paper that can be posted in a prominent place.

Getting Down to the Nitty-gritty

Because our marriage history contained some major offenses, we found it necessary to develop several standards that specifically spoke to those dicey issues. This may be true for you as well. For example, it was important for us to have a standard that reflected forgiveness and an agreement never to dredge up the past in order to hurt each other. Of course, it was easy to find Bible verses that matched with standards of forgiveness and mercy.

Sometimes you may wish to start with a Bible verse and write a standard based on it. Or you can start with an idea and find the appropriate Scripture to reflect the standard. Continue the process of developing your marriage standards and finding corresponding verses until you have a comprehensive list of what matters most to God regarding your relationship. Look at causes of past pain, such as infidelity, rage, or dishonesty, and compose standards that address those issues specifically. This is an important key to not repeating past mistakes.

Nehemiah took a similar course with the Israelites once he brought them back into alignment with God's laws, convinced them to stop taking advantage of each other, and ended the repetition of inappropriate behavior.

Then I summoned the priests and made the nobles and officials take an oath to do what they had promised. I also shook out the folds of my robe and said, "In this way may God shake out of their house and possessions anyone who does not keep this promise. So may such a person be shaken out and emptied!"

At this the whole assembly said, "Amen," and praised the LORD. And the people did as they had promised. (Neh. 5:12–13)

When Nehemiah shook out the folds of his robe, he was making a strong symbolic statement about what would happen if the people returned to their old patterns of behavior in blatant disregard of God's commands. Part of the challenge of making certain your marriage remains focused on biblically based standards is to find creative ways to regularly integrate them into your marriage and family. It's not enough to write them down and never revisit them. After you've developed your standards, it's important to continue reviewing them so they remain as your foundation. In order to do this, you may find it helpful to regularly engage in the following activities.

Integrating Standards into Your Marriage

- Pray over your standards weekly. Allow God to examine your heart for areas that may be out of alignment with His Word and to reveal the ways your behavior needs to change.
- Use these standards to help you make wise decisions and to stay focused on what matters most.
- Meditate on and memorize the Scripture verses you selected for your standards.

- Ask a trusted Christian couple to hold you accountable to fulfilling your marriage standards. Give them a copy of your standards and your permission to ask about the ways your marriage is growing, changing, or struggling.

Once you've developed your marriage standards, commit them to God and promise each other to hold tightly to what you've agreed upon for the remainder of your lives. Consider a prayer of dedication as you agree to adhere to these commitments. From time to time, you'll find it necessary to amend your standards as your relationship deepens and as you encounter trials and circumstances you haven't dealt with before.

Basing our marriage on God's standards has undeniably transformed our relationship the second time around. It has taken work, discussion, practice, failure, and a lot of prayer. However, we eventually noticed that our greatest concerns were no longer about getting our own way but about making certain we both respected and honored God's ways. As time has passed and we've learned how to cover our marriage standards with prayer, God has blown the lid off of our relationship. Integrating prayer into *every* aspect of our marriage has allowed for the complete restoration and redemption of past pain and has launched our marriage into brand-new territory. Effectively, creatively, and faithfully integrating prayer into your own marriage will be the subject of the next chapter.

Prayer to Align Your Standards

God, we each brought our own standards into our marriage, and some of them weren't in alignment with Your Word. We want to make a change. We desire to base our marriage on the principles and promises in the Bible. Reveal the areas of our relationship You want us to focus on. Lead us to the verses You want as our foundation. May Your Holy Spirit align our hearts and minds with Yours so that we come to agreements that honor You. We believe our marriage will be restored when we steadfastly base all our interactions on the standards found in Your Word. In Jesus' name we pray. Amen.

For a Marriage on the Mend

Come Together

Take some time to pray together, search God's Word, and write at least two standards for your marriage. Don't try to accomplish this in one sitting. You may wish to use the samples of standards from this chapter and combine them with some of your own. Each standard should be accompanied by a corresponding Bible verse or passage. After you've written your marriage standards, pray over them, giving God the opportunity to change or refine them further. When you're ready, print out the final standards and corresponding verses, frame them, and place them prominently in your home. You may wish to engage in a time of commitment and communion together as well. This is a memorable spiritual event for families to engage in and can become a treasured part of your spiritual legacy.

Questions to Consider

1. What are some of the standards you brought into your marriage regarding the roles and responsibilities of husbands and wives? What about your standards regarding spending habits? Handling conflict? Cultural traditions? Where or with whom did these originate?

2. What or who is the current focus of your marriage? Explain your answer. (Note: The answer will likely tell you upon what or whom your marriage is based.)

3. Skim back over Nehemiah 4. What do you notice regarding Nehemiah's determination and attitude toward the opposition he faced?

4. How might Nehemiah's approach to his problems apply to the restoration of your marriage?

5. As you continue adding positive and negative life events to your timeline, can you identify the ways biblical standards might have stabilized your relationship during tough times? How did the standards you possessed prior to marrying play into the struggles with your spouse?

Chapter 8

Using Prayer as a Power Tool

But when Sanballat, Tobiah, the Arabs, the Ammonites and the people of Ashdod heard that the repairs to Jerusalem's walls had gone ahead and that the gaps were being closed, they were very angry. They all plotted together to come and fight against Jerusalem and stir up trouble against it. But we prayed to our God. (Neh. 4:7–9)

Nehemiah knew exactly how to deal with the circumstances threatening to interrupt the rebuilding of Jerusalem's walls. When challenges arose, he fought off his foes and silenced their accusations by praying and continuing the work God called him to complete. Throughout the book of Nehemiah, we see evidence that of all the tools in his tool belt, prayer was by far his most powerful and valuable resource.

They were all trying to frighten us, thinking, "Their hands will get too weak for the work, and it will not be completed." But I prayed, "Now strengthen my hands." (Neh. 6:9)

Like Nehemiah, you must make intercession an essential "power tool" that you use regularly to keep your marriage in consistent alignment with God's standards. Your prayer life will be most effective and life-changing when it is a part of *everything* you do. Like

breathing, prayer must become something you engage in constantly—
almost subconsciously and without hesitation or reservation.

In our work as marriage missionaries, we host a worldwide prayer
line on WAPN Radio in Holly Hill, Florida. When God led us to
WAPN, we couldn't believe there was a Christian radio station in
our area wholly dedicated to two things: preaching the Word and
praying for people.

During our broadcasts, people from all over the nation call in
for prayer regarding the restoration of their marriages and families.
Praying with people in pain is a sacred experience we never take for
granted.

What seems to be missing from most of the people who call is the
desire or the know-how to pray together as a couple. Many first generation Christians have been told to pray but have never been shown how.

If you want to take your prayer life to the next level and learn how
to pray together, this chapter can help. But beware: these tools are
not for the faint of heart. When you pray together, you give God permission to radically transform your marriage. There are few things
that move the heart of God more than spouses who pray together.

Facing Each Day with Prayer

As is often the case, it took a major crisis for Penny and me to
realize the true power of praying together. Several months after we
remarried, a frightening incident took place at the school where I
was teaching. In the midst of an ongoing investigation and a lot of
red tape, I suggested we pray together before I left for school one
morning. Afterward, as the miles passed on my commute, I felt an
overwhelming sense of God's peace permeating my heart and mind.
That peace remained with me through the day, and the difficult
circumstances I faced at school got ironed out much more quickly
than I anticipated. When I shared this with Penny that evening, she
told me she had experienced the same sense of calm.

Prior to this incident, Penny and I prayed together once a week but not daily. We decided to pray together again the next morning. Every morning for the rest of that week, I placed my arm around Penny's shoulder, and we spent two or three minutes in prayer before I went out the front door. My prayer went something like this: "Father, we ask You to join us this day. We need Your presence in our lives. Please provide for our every need and protect us from the Enemy. Help us to follow You wherever You lead as we trust You. In Jesus' name. Amen."

It was that simple. As a result of what God did that week, we made a marriage-altering decision to never leave the house in the morning without praying together. That was years ago. To this day, praying together remains an integral part of our morning routine.

 Using Prayer as a Power Tool · *4:42 minutes*

Making Your Marriage a Prayer Priority

When God first began reconciling us, Clint and I lived more than three thousand miles apart on opposite coasts of the United States. In an effort to grow closer despite the miles between us, we decided to pray together over the phone once a week. Every Sunday, we took turns calling each other and sharing our prayer requests. Prayer bridged the miles between us in indescribable ways.

When we remarried, we thought it would be wise to keep a good thing going. So we continue to meet on Sunday nights and share our praises and prayer requests. This gives us the opportunity to check in with each other about any concerns that surfaced during the week. We also review our requests from the previous week and discuss the ways God answered our prayers. (More on weekly prayer and devotional time in chapter 10.)

One of the greatest challenges for a reconciling couple is the tendency for each person to point the finger at their spouse for the changes that need to occur instead of praying for him or her. Just after Clint and I remarried, my friend Annie gave me a piece of advice I've never forgotten. She said, "It's not your job to be the Holy Spirit in Clint's life or to try to make him change."

I wish I could say I've always heeded Annie's words, but at the start I was definitely guilty of determining the changes I thought Clint should make. In time, I realized that praying for, blessing, and affirming Clint would have a far more positive impact on our marriage than any changes I tried to force on him.

I'm not alone in my tendency to figure out ways to modify my mate. Many people come to us with a litany of things they want to change about their spouse. As a result of the constant nagging and fault-finding, walls are erected in these marriages that seem impossible to break down.

Save yourself a lot of heartache. Instead of spending all your energy trying to change your spouse, ask God how He wants to change *you* and how He wants you to pray for your spouse. Use Scripture to guide your prayers. Seek to affirm your spouse in spite of your differences; encourage his or her varied interests, hobbies, and ways of doing things, even if some of them frustrate you. Pay close attention to what's important to your mate. Taking a genuine interest in the things that are meaningful to your spouse and faithfully praying for him or her will create new connection points in your relationship. One of the greatest gifts you can give your spouse is the freedom to be different from you. Even if you don't always understand what makes your mate tick, you can find creative and meaningful ways to demonstrate love.

One practical way I pray for Clint is by using one of our wedding photos as my Bible bookmark. On the back of the photo, I place a sticky note that contains a prayer list for him. Every day when I open my Bible, I reflect on the priceless gift of being remarried, and I remember to pray for Clint. As I sense God answering prayers or making changes, I remove the old note and replace it with a new one. Each time I do so, I ask God to show me how *He* sees Clint and how *He* wants me to pray for him.

Another way I pray for Clint is to get up before he does and sit in the recliner where he meets with God. I suppose in a very tangible way, sitting in that special place shifts my perspective. When I pray in his chair, I ask God to reveal how I can best support Clint and become a more suitable helpmate. Sometimes I'll just place my hand on his Bible or devotional books, praying as the Spirit leads. At other times, I'll pray for God to establish, anoint, and bless the projects Clint is working on for our ministry.

One of my most effective and thorough ways to pray for Clint, our marriage, and my role as his wife is to assemble a prayer scrapbook. I take a blank book, and on each page I glue a different photo of Clint or of the two of us. At the top of every page, I write down a particular area of concern such as family relationships, physical health, serving God, spiritual growth, and so on. Once the photos are glued in place, I ask God for a Scripture verse or passage to claim regarding that page's specific focus, and I inscribe that verse next to each photo. I use the prayer scrapbook to write down requests and record answers for the entire year. I also note the changes God makes in both of us.

Flipping through the pages of those prayer scrapbooks now, I'm astounded by the ways God responded to my prayers and by the changes He has made. Those scrapbooks are treasured mementos and undeniable evidence of the powerful tool prayer has been in restoring Clint and me.

Creating a prayer scrapbook is also a great way to rebuild family unity and nurture the reconciliation between family members. Allow each child to create a page. Participation from the rest of the family creates more buy-in and is a profound way to trace God's hand over all of your lives.

Prayer with a Guarantee

During our first two years of remarriage, Penny and I conducted a mini-investigation on the topic and practice of prayer. We spent time searching the Scriptures during our individual quiet times. Together, we read books about prayer and discussed our opinions about what we were reading. Our curiosity grew as to how others organized their prayer lives and whether or not they used lists, journals, or other methods to keep track of prayer requests and answers. We discovered that there are unlimited ways to approach, organize, and utilize prayer. What matters most is that we make praying for each other and our marriage a high priority.

During this same time, author and pastor Rick Warren released his book, *The Purpose Driven Life*, and we committed to participating in its forty-day program at our church. Each evening, we read a chapter of Warren's book together. As we sat at the table that first night, we decided it might be a good idea to compose a prayer to use throughout our forty-day journey. Penny grabbed a pencil and paper and jotted down our thoughts as we talked. By the end of the evening, we'd composed this prayer:

Heavenly Father,
We surrender this day to You. We surrender ourselves and all the resources You've given us to accomplish Your purpose. Reveal to us Your purpose for our lives and expose the obstacles of sin that keep us from living out that purpose. Lord, release Your power within us to do the right thing, not only with those we love but those we dislike as well. Help us to be a vessel through which Jesus shines. We surrender our minds, hearts, souls, bodies, and wills to Your sovereign

authority. We are Yours, Lord. May we be closer to You by the day's end. In Jesus' name we pray. Amen.

We each wrote down that prayer, tucked it into our Bibles, and prayed it every day for forty days. Almost immediately, a dramatic shift occurred in our relationships with God and each other. At first, neither of us could put a finger on what was happening. But over time we realized the prayer we'd written guaranteed a "yes" response from God. We hadn't asked God for tangible things, detailed plans, or material possessions as we had so often in the past. Instead, we surrendered all those things to God daily, asking Him to have His way in our hearts. God will *always* agree to prayers like that.

As a result of this discovery, we created a list of simple prayer phrases. If you're willing to submit yourselves fully to God, we guarantee that, simple as they may seem, these prayers will be answered with God's enthusiastic nod. Ever since we started praying this way, our faith has deepened, our marriage has improved, and God has given us a desire to trust Him to an even greater degree.

Prayer with a Guarantee · *3:47 minutes*

- -
Prayers with a Guarantee
- -

Please give us Your mind and wisdom so we think like You in every circumstance.

Reveal Yourself to us through Your Word and show us Your perfect will for us.

Mold us, shape us, and transform us into Your image.

Meet us in the midst of this conflict. Show us the tangible ways we can honor You throughout this ordeal.

Reveal any sins that clutter our minds and hinder our hearts from hearing You or seeing our relationship from Your perspective.

Change our hearts so that we're more forgiving, merciful, humble, and gentle.

Surround us with wise counsel, godly support, and opportunities for healthy fellowship.

Please don't give us anything that will bring us more pleasure than You.

Cutting Through Everyday Conflict

Before you married, did anyone sit you down and tell you there would be times of disagreement in your relationship? Most couples never imagined they'd be at such great odds.

During our first marriage, Penny and I didn't know we should proactively prepare for conflict. We were so caught up with being in love and experiencing the wonderful aspects of our honeymoon phase that we didn't know how to handle our first major disagreement. Neither of us had ever seen conflict play out in a healthy way between spouses. Out of ignorance, we reacted to each other from our emotions, opinions, upbringing, and selfishness instead of managing our problems with God's help. Our priorities were all about getting our own needs met, not about serving each other, and so we became a part of the divorce statistic we're now so passionate about reducing.

Back then, it never occurred to us to use prayer as a power tool to work through our differences. Today we know better than to repeat past mistakes. At first we weren't sure how to approach prayer in our marriage, but we have discovered that immediately calling on God as our advocate and judge has to be our first line of defense against division. Many times, in the midst of a disagreement, one of us has stopped and prayed something like, "Lord, help us! We're struggling and we need Your wisdom and opinion. Meet us in the middle of this conflict and show us Your better way."

At other times, we have disengaged from a conversation that was turning sour in order to move apart and pray alone. Through these experiences, we've learned that when we include God and seek His righteousness and wisdom through prayer, He consistently settles our disputes long before things get out of hand.

While Penny and I share many similarities and common interests, we are very different people. You could say that Penny is a psalm and I am a proverb. Penny is expressive: a true visionary who thrives when she's thrown by the seat of her pants into a challenging situation. I am a linear thinker who operates best when there's a plan laid out or a specific model to follow. These differences make our marriage interesting as well as challenging.

After many opportunities to practice handling our differences through prayer, we created a simple diagram to help other couples prayerfully approach and resolve their differences. Combined with prayer, the Gradients of Agreement Diagram will help you negotiate when you don't see eye-to-eye. That way, you can maintain peace and harmony in your home despite your unique personalities and differences.

Gradients of Agreement · *5:10 minutes*

Gradients of Agreement Diagram

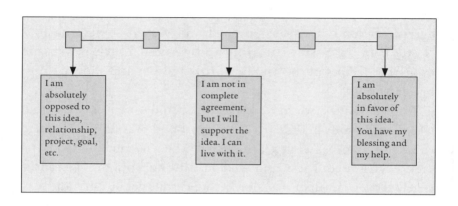

| I am absolutely opposed to this idea, relationship, project, goal, etc. | I am not in complete agreement, but I will support the idea. I can live with it. | I am absolutely in favor of this idea. You have my blessing and my help. |

Think of this diagram as a visual tool you carry in your mind to help clarify where you are on the gradient scale when a disagreement is brewing. If used prayerfully, this diagram can help you clarify and express your thoughts, opinions, and feelings. Here are some general guidelines we've developed in relation to using it to bring clarity and resolve conflict.

- If you find yourselves at opposite ends of the gradient, stop the conversation and cool off. Set another time to restart the discussion after you've had the chance to pray and figure out your feelings. This gives God the opportunity to help you gain some perspective.
- The diagram and your disagreement work in conjunction with your individual time with God. It's much easier for your spouse to trust your ideas and opinions when he or she knows you're seeking God's counsel every day in His Word and prayer.
- If one of you is completely opposed to an idea, project, relationship, decision, purchase, etc., and your spouse feels the

exact opposite about it, wait, pray, and seek God. Ask Him to use the Holy Spirit, the Bible, wise counsel, and each other to confirm whether or not you should move forward. Mutually submit to God and each other. Don't forge ahead unless you both feel God has said so and you're fairly close together on the gradient scale.

· If you are in the "I can live with it" box regarding something your spouse is proposing, discuss the kinds of support you will give. It's never fair to harden your heart and pull away from your spouse because you aren't in *absolute* agreement with him or her. Be clear and specific about your concerns, but be willing to support your spouse. Remember, you're called to serve one another and put your spouse's needs above yours, even when you might not understand him or her.

· Even when you're both in full agreement, you must be certain God is in favor of what you want to do. This process takes time and prayer. You should never let impulsivity prematurely move you ahead of God or lead you outside His will.

· Sometimes it's helpful to bring tough conflicts before an accountability/prayer partner for wise counsel.

· God will often use your spouse to confirm the direction of an idea, project, or goal. Be open to having God speak to you through your spouse. This takes practice, patience, and trust.

· Always be open to a change of heart. God can change the hearts and minds of His people. Through prayer, place your frustration, hope, and spouse in God's hands, and keep asking Him how He wants to change *your* heart.

If disagreements are handled in a way that honors God, every single one can serve to display His glory and help strengthen your marriage. If God truly is an integral part of your union, He must be invited to participate in your disagreements, and He must be given a say in what transpires. When allowed to intervene, the Holy Spirit will absorb all the excess pressure, tension, and stress involved in the conflict and its resolution. When you allow prayer to cut through conflict, you open the door for God to enter in and change everything.

Nehemiah's impulse to pray through every challenge sets a high standard in your own ongoing work of restoration. Bailing out of the rebuilding project was not an option for Nehemiah, and walking out on your marriage isn't an option for you. No matter what transpires, it's never appropriate to dangle threats of separation or divorce over one another. Whether you're angry, confused, weak, tired, frustrated, discouraged, or doubtful, looking for a way out isn't the answer. Instead, exercise your option to pray. If we, as husbands and wives, have any impulses during the restoration process, let us be impulsive to pray immediately, fervently, frequently, and honestly.

Our dear friends Chuck and Micki Ann have learned a thing or two about using prayer to cut through conflict and draw them closer together. Having started the restoration process many years ago, they developed a simple nonverbal cue that serves as an immediate call to prayer. A hand extended palms-up, and all conversation or activity stops. Immediately they join hands and pray.

When we interviewed them about the role of prayer in their marriage and family, Chuck made the following memorable statement: "It's not so much that prayer automatically changes the nature of our circumstances, but more importantly, prayer humbles and changes *my* heart toward the circumstance."

Over the years, the two have trained up their children in the way of prayer. Intercession is woven so tightly into the fabric of their family that they dedicated one entire room in their house as a special place for prayer. Clint and I had the privilege of assisting in the construction of this prayer room and were greatly inspired by their need and passion for prayer. Intercession is as paramount to their survival as bread and water. That is how it should be.

Severing Your Strongholds

One of the challenges of restoring your relationship is dealing with conflicts from the past that may unexpectedly revisit you. We'll discuss this in more detail in the next chapter, but for now, we must note an important point: deeply rooted strongholds are often at the source of unbecoming behaviors and choices. Prayer is the power tool that can slice through these strongholds so they are no longer a source of division.

A simple definition of a stronghold is "an unhealthy or skewed pattern of thinking or relating based on deception." Anything having to do with deception is always a weapon Satan wields against God's people. However, God has given us a counter-weapon that can obliterate all strongholds.

> Though we live in the world, we do not wage war as the world does. The weapons we fight with are not the weapons of the world. On the contrary, they have divine power to demolish strongholds. We demolish arguments and every pretension that sets itself up against the knowledge of God, and we take captive every thought to make it obedient to Christ. (2 Cor. 10:3–5)

Strongholds cause us to think and act in ways that divert us from experiencing true wholeness in Christ. They also keep us from receiving God's full measure of blessing. Strongholds can make our relationships with God and others grow stagnant because they're based on faulty reasoning, false arguments, and the Enemy's lies. For example, many people admit to viewing God as a tyrannical ruler who only exists to angrily hand down punishment. As a result, they get stuck living with a sense of guilt or shame that hovers over their lives and keeps them from fully experiencing God's grace and love.

In marriage, a stronghold often masquerades as a repeat offense. Repeat offenses occur in every marriage, but they pose an even greater threat to couples working through the process of restoration. When an issue repeatedly resurfaces, an underlying stronghold is likely at work, and it can take a while to unmask it. Strongholds are hidden far beneath the surface of ongoing conflict because Satan does not want his deceptive tactics exposed. Prayer is a critical element in accurately identifying and demolishing every stronghold.

Joe and Gerri Begay were raised on the Navajo Reservation in Arizona. We met them after one of our speaking engagements in Farmington, New Mexico. "Joe and I got married before I finished high school," explained Gerri. "After four kids, years of repeated rage, and Joe's addiction to alcohol, we divorced. For the sake of our children, we eventually reconciled and remarried after having our fifth child. However, when we hit conflict again, we brought up offenses from the past. After our second divorce, I lost hope. I started leaving my children and hanging out at the border town bars."

Joe continued their story.

"It was after the failure of our second marriage that we individually invited Christ to end our addictions to alcohol and to stop all the other repeat offenses that had torn us apart in the past. We vowed to each other that we would never, never bring up past offenses again. At the altar of a local church, Gerri and I got on our knees and asked God to take over control of our lives."

Shortly thereafter, Joe and Gerri remarried each other for the third and final time.

"We started using prayer to restore our marriage by remembering to regularly thank God for saving us and bringing us back together. Eventually we learned how to use prayer to resolve our disagreements. Even now, when difficulties arise in our relationship, we take a 'strife break,' find a verse or passage from the Bible that applies to our situation, and pray together about the problem.

"We are living proof that the way to victory over alcohol, bitterness, and hatred is through Jesus Christ."[4]

Today, Joe and Gerri pastor a thriving church in Chinle, Arizona. During our time together, they told us about how the strongholds of alcohol, drugs, and gambling are spreading across the Navajo Nation. To help others find freedom, Joe and Gerri make themselves available for open prayer ministry after each worship service. We were humbled to witness them in action when we visited their church. It was plain to see why they will spend the rest of their lives leading others to victory in Christ through prayer.

Getting Specific with God • *5:11 minutes*

Getting Specific with God

In her book *Prayer Essentials for Living in His Presence*, Sylvia Gunter writes, "Every family needs some measure of release from generational bondages. Maybe we have never thought about how we pass down from generation to generation a family stronghold or altar at which we bow down. Think about evidences of family shrines: 'The Smiths always . . .' or 'The Smiths are sixth generation . . .' Or, perhaps a bondage exists to a behavior that repeats itself generation after generation, for example, anger, sexual sin, or alcoholism."[5]

Gunter goes on to state that the cycle of generational strongholds can be broken through prayer and that it is essential to also ask God to establish new lines of blessing for the coming generations in your family line.

Getting free from strongholds will require you to get specific with God. One of the tools we teach couples is how to write
prayers together that focus on ending the cycle of repeat offenses
and shattering strongholds. The Holy Spirit can break a stronghold immediately—we've seen it happen. However, some strongholds require a *process of prayer* to stop their destructive cycle.
Writing prayers together, praying fervently, and believing God's
Word will sever strongholds more effectively and permanently
than anything else.

If you've come up against the same issue over and over again,
we suggest you join together to compose a prayer specifically tailored to identify the stronghold, expose it, and tear it down. To
help you better understand this process, we've written a step-by-
step guide and a sample prayer to break a stronghold many marriages are facing today: money.

Let's assume you have recurring arguments over finances. This
stronghold will frequently manifest in repeated offenses over
things like spending and saving habits, budgets, lack of adequate
financial resources, impulsive purchases, or inconsistent tithing,
to name a few. These things may even be traced back through
several generations. Let this step-by-step guide help you grasp
the concept of using prayer as a power tool to tear down that
stronghold.

Step One: Ask the Holy Spirit to expose the true nature of the
stronghold. Don't try to discuss the issue or write a prayer without first asking God to reveal the root of the matter. This process may take some time. Bring the stronghold and its manifestation (the repeated offenses) to God together, and ask Him
to shed His light and truth on it. Locate a verse or passage of
Scripture to claim over this problem, and use it to help you compose a prayer.

Step Two: Take turns contributing ideas, words, and sentences to form a prayer that expresses both of your hearts. The prayer should focus on tearing down the stronghold *and* replacing your unhealthy thinking patterns and/or behaviors with godly attitudes and actions. This second part is essential so you don't fill the void with another stronghold.

Step Three: After you write the prayer, make copies of it and post it in several places (home, office, mirror, car, journal, Bible) as a reminder to pray it regularly with a believing heart. Be patient; some strongholds extend back through several generations, and it may take some time to completely uproot and destroy them.

Step Four: Pray *until.* That is, keep praying, asking, and knocking on God's door until the stronghold is removed and you experience a change in the dynamics of your relationship with Him and with each other. You may sense this liberation and deliverance immediately or over time. Remember, God's timelines and processes are as important as the outcomes, especially when it comes to matters of the heart.

Step Five: Throughout the process, give thanks for all the ways God answers your prayer, tears down the stronghold, and gives you victory. Observe how He works, and praise Him for new thoughts and behavior patterns that are grounded in the Word.

The following is a sample prayer we wrote based on this step-by-step process. If you're currently living in bondage to the stronghold of money, you're welcome to use this prayer. However, we also encourage you to ask the Holy Spirit for His guidance in composing a prayer that addresses your specific behavior patterns and the ways in which these things need to be exposed and uprooted.

Sample Prayer to Break the Stronghold of Money

Holy Spirit, You've revealed to us that our repeated arguments over money are really a deeply rooted stronghold.
Luke 16:13 says, "No one can serve two masters. Either you
will hate the one and love the other, or you will be devoted
to the one and despise the other. You cannot serve both God
and money."

Our marriage has been a slave to money. We confess our
sins of unhealthy thinking and behavior to You and ask for
Your forgiveness and cleansing. We specifically ask, in Jesus'
name, that You completely sever the stronghold of money
in our marriage. Grant us freedom from what has bound
us and kept us from experiencing more of Your blessings.
Break the mental and soul ties of this stronghold over past
and future generations. Set our family free from living
under the impact and bondage of deception. Replace our
ungodly thoughts and actions with those that respect You
and edify each other. Guide us to answers in Your Word so
we honor You with the funds You've given us. Show us Your
way of dealing with every area of our finances, including the
faithful giving of tithes and offerings. Temper our impulsive purchases. Show us biblical, wise, and tangible ways
to save, spend, and share our resources. Please provide for
the needs of our family, and enable us to become faithful
stewards. Help us strike a balance and blend our differences
together so we come into a financial agreement that is not
our plan but Your plan. In Jesus' name. Amen.

Rebuilding Intimacy Through Prayer

We would be extremely remiss if we didn't discuss the vital role of
prayer in restoring and rebuilding physical and emotional intimacy

in your marriage. Most couples who have been through a crisis, separation, or divorce are starting from scratch in all facets of marital intimacy. That was certainly the case for Clint and me. Intimacy was grossly lacking in our first marriage, and we were starting at ground zero when we remarried.

The thought of developing physical intimacy with Clint sparked anxiety in me. Although neither of us had remarried during our years apart, we had both crossed over appropriate sexual boundaries with others. We asked God to forgive us for these sins and fully disclosed them to each other, but we had no idea how this aspect of our past would play out in our remarriage.

Many couples today face the same scenario. Infidelity, sexual addiction, or other sins have occurred outside of marriage and threaten to dash any hope for healing. But Clint and I tell couples that if God healed all the mistakes and pain of *our* pasts, He is willing and able do the same for them. God wants to heal your marriage and make it whole. Redeeming every part of our sinfulness and brokenness is the reason Jesus came to earth. Here's an example of how prayer helped Clint and me over the intimacy hurdle.

Due to the details involved in our reconciliation, Clint only had about eight weeks to put his home up for sale in Florida, pack his belongings, and drive to California in time for our wedding. So not only was there an eleven-year gap in our relationship and indiscretions in our pasts, but we didn't get to spend time together until just five days before we remarried. There were few opportunities to begin building intimacy prior to our remarriage. But we firmly relied on God for what seemed impossible.

Three days before our wedding, we invited our marriage mentors, Dale and Colleen, to visit us at what would soon be our home as husband and wife. We planned to have them cleanse and bless each room of the house, believing with us that prayer would be the catalyst to create, establish, and nurture intimacy. The four of us spent the evening walking from room to room, cleansing and blessing each area. In the living room, we prayed for things like fellowship and times of rest. In the kitchen, we prayed about our health and the breaking of bread together. In the bathrooms, we prayed for our image to mirror Christ's. On the front porch, we prayed for protection in all our coming and going and for nothing divisive to ever enter our marriage or home. This continued throughout each room as well as the front and backyard.

When we all walked into the master bedroom, I felt a lump forming in my throat. Tears of fear and anxiety welled up and spilled down my cheeks. With the four of us kneeling together at the bedside, we prayed fervently for the establishment of sexual and emotional intimacy. We prayed for cleansing from the past and complete healing for our future. It was a time Clint and I will always treasure. We're convinced that the prayers offered to God that night continue to be answered to this day.

Prayer is the backbone for reestablishing intimacy. Praying for emotional, physical, and spiritual intimacy should become a regular part of your marital prayer life and must not be neglected at any time during the remainder of your lives together.

Prayer should be a part of *everything* you do. For example, have you ever considered praying about the sexual part of your marriage? Have you asked God to show you how to be physically intimate? How to please one another in the bedroom? Have you prayed that your times of sexual intimacy would reflect His perfect and holy design for marriage? Have you prayed prior to or after making love?

Some couples don't feel comfortable praying these kinds of prayers together or aloud at first. That's understandable. If that's the case, pray silently on your own. It doesn't matter *how* you pray—it matters *that* you pray and believe God is able to completely restore intimacy in all facets of your marriage. If you're uncertain how to begin praying about this vital area, here are a few prayer prompts to assist you.

Sample Prayer Prompts for Establishing Intimacy

Erase any prior images or memories that are a consequence of our sins.

Increase our desire and passion for each other.

Heal the areas of insecurity and vulnerability in us.

Show us how to please one another and be sensitive to each other's needs.

Cleanse us from the sinful ways we damaged intimacy, and help us rebuild it in our marriage.

Restore and protect the fidelity in our marriage, and let no one and nothing come between us.

Teach us how to know and respect each other's areas of insecurity and vulnerability when it comes to self-image and sexuality.

Enable us to communicate our emotional and physical needs without the fear of rejection.

Give us the words to affirm each other's inward and outward beauty.

Faithfully using prayer as a power tool in *every* area of your marriage will help you make great progress toward complete wholeness. Through prayer, you can successfully navigate all your past and present trials and draw closer to God and to each other. Prayer is indispensable. Every promise in God's Word is activated through steadfast, fervent, and authentic prayer.

Prayer for Establishing a Prayerful Marriage

Lord, teach us to faithfully pray for our marriage and for each other. Show us ways we can integrate powerful, effective, and restorative prayer into our lives. We believe prayer is an important key to our complete healing. Through Your Holy Spirit, remind us to pray together about everything. Teach us how to seek Your presence and make Your eternal priorities our own.

Prepare and equip us for times of disagreement. We desire to handle conflict in a way that pleases You and strengthens us. Broaden our perspective during disagreements so we see more than just our own needs and desires. Bless us with what we're lacking.

Show us creative ways to develop and deepen emotional, physical, and spiritual intimacy. Grant us the wisdom to expose and sever the strongholds that hinder us. Pardon all our sins and shortcomings, and grant us the mercy to forgive each other without condition. Cover our relationship with Your sovereign hand of protection from any attempts to divide our family. We ask all these things of You in faith, believing You'll hear our prayers and respond. In Jesus' name we pray. Amen.

For a Marriage on the Mend

Write a Prayer

Think about a repeat offense in your marriage. Ask God to reveal the underlying stronghold and apply the steps outlined in this chapter to compose a prayer together. Your goal is to expose and tear down the stronghold that hinders you. Take turns offering ideas, words, and sentences until you've written a prayer that reflects both of your hearts.

Questions to Consider

1. What are some of the ideas about prayer in this chapter and/or in the book of Nehemiah that spark your interest?

2. What or who is hindering you from spending more time in prayer individually and with your spouse? How can you remedy this?

3. What do you notice about the confession of sin recorded in Nehemiah 9:1–2?

4. Is there any evidence of generational strongholds in your own life? If so, what are they?
5. Take out your marriage timeline. How might prayer have positively impacted the negative life events you've listed on the timeline thus far?

Chapter 9

Guarding Your Marriage Gates

I said to [the Jewish leaders], "You see the trouble we are in: Jerusalem lies in ruins, and its gates have been burned with fire." (Neh. 2:17)

Enemy attacks were often concentrated at the gates of a city because they were the most vulnerable points of entry. Nehemiah's written account of Jerusalem's restoration indicates that a great deal of the rebuilding process had to do with making necessary repairs to the gates, most of which had been burned by fire. The third chapter of Nehemiah contains a vivid description of the labor and teamwork necessary to completely restore the gates and set them in place. According to biblical commentators, there were approximately forty-five teams of workers on the wall, with at least forty workers on each team.

Although the division of roles and responsibilities between men and women was normally distinct, the urgency of the task at hand allowed women and girls to participate in the rebuilding (Neh. 3:12). Not only were females expected to participate, but many people were required to labor outside of their normal areas of expertise. For example, perfumers and goldsmiths left the comfort zones of their intricate handiwork to lift bulky building materials (Neh. 3:8).

Guarding the Gates of Your Marriage, Part 1 · *4:45 minutes*

During our trip to Israel in 2006, we had the opportunity to walk around each of the gates in modern-day Jerusalem. Each gate served an important purpose in the everyday operations of the city. But while commentators agree that these gates tell the gospel story, they also provide an important analogy for maintaining a healthy marriage. Carefully guarding what each gate symbolizes will ensure the ongoing protection of your relationship.

Join us on a tour of Jerusalem's gates based on the third chapter of Nehemiah. Traveling clockwise around the city, we'll stop at each gate in order to apply its history and significance to marriage. Don't hesitate to also include your relationships with your children in what you discover.

As in the rest of this book, we'll be using the New International Version (NIV). Other Bible translations may refer to these gates by different names. However, their history, purpose, and symbolism remain the same in every version.

The Sheep Gate

> Eliashib the high priest and his fellow priests went to work and rebuilt the Sheep Gate. (Neh. 3:1)

The first gate on our tour is the Sheep Gate, which was located in the northeast corner of Jerusalem near the temple. It was through this gate that animals were brought to the temple for sacrifice. It is no surprise that Eliashib and the other priests concentrated on this gate first, since their primary responsibility was to sacrifice animals in the temple to atone for the sins of the people.

In the New Testament, we read that Jesus Christ became the sacrifice for all our sins. "The next day John saw Jesus coming toward him and said, 'Look, the Lamb of God, who takes away the sin of the world!'" (John 1:29). Through Christ's redemptive work on the cross, our sins are forgiven and we are reconciled to God. When we're reconciled to God, we can be reconciled to each other as well.

Scholar and commentator J. Vernon McGee writes, "Personally, I think the Lord Jesus came in at the Sheep Gate every time he entered the city except for at the Triumphal Entry."[6] McGee speculates that when Jesus was arrested and led out to be crucified, He was brought out through that gate as well.

In light of this, the Sheep Gate speaks of several necessities for a healthy marriage. Of primary importance is the role of Christ in your relationship with your spouse (and with your children). Reconciliation is not about following a recipe for restoration but about following Jesus. He sacrificed His life for us, once and for all.

Guarding this gate of your marriage and family means protecting the time you spend with God every day and staying in the center of His will. Be mindful to keep Christ as the center of your life at all times. No person, possession, or responsibility should ever take precedence over your relationship with Him.

The Sheep Gate also reminds us that relationships demand self-sacrifice. Jesus stated, "Whoever wants to be my disciple must deny themselves and take up their cross daily and follow me" (Luke 9:23). We are called to follow Christ's example.

More than any other relationship, marriage requires sacrificing your own desires and serving your spouse's needs before your own. I (Penny) admit there are times when I'm selfish and must get on my face before God and repeat, "I choose You and I choose Clint." This phrase is my way of surrendering to God's desires and to serving Clint's needs before I satisfy my own.

Consider using a similar phrase of surrender, or perhaps some visual image, when faced with the struggle to sacrifice your own needs for God, your spouse, and your children. When you desire to have your way so badly that you can taste it, get on your knees and ask God to feed you with the bread of His presence and the water of His Word.

During a mission trip, God powerfully reminded Clint and me that marriage requires us to deny ourselves whether we feel like it or not. We were near the end of our journey and weary of life on the road. Traveling together for forty days has its challenges, and it's easy to become lax in serving each other. One afternoon, as we were driving down a lonely Louisiana highway, Clint suddenly blurted, "Look, there's Jesus!" In the distance was a long-haired man dressed in a white robe.

We blinked in disbelief. As we got closer, we could see that the man was dragging a huge cross along the side of the highway. As we drove by, he raised his hand and called out, "God bless you!" Seeing him drag that heavy cross down that forlorn road etched into our minds the reality of what Jesus requires in a way we won't forget.

Your marriage and relationships with other family members will require frequent stops at the Sheep Gate to remember the sacred sacrifice that the spotless Lamb of God made for you.

The Fish Gate

> The Fish Gate was rebuilt by the sons of Hassenaah. They laid its beams and put its doors and bolts and bars in place. (Neh. 3:3)

Continuing our tour around the northern wall of the city, we come to the Fish Gate. Through this gate, merchants brought in their catches from the Mediterranean Sea, the Sea of Galilee, the Jordan River, and other nearby waters. The Fish Gate symbolizes the call of Jesus to His disciples. "'Come, follow me,' Jesus said, 'and I will send you out to fish for people'" (Matt. 4:19). Once we're saved to eternal life, we're expected to be witnesses of God's love to the rest of the world.

It was through the love of several married couples that I (Penny) was wooed back into the folds of the faith many years ago. These couples, whom I met through my job as a school principal, tenderly took me under their wings and loved me despite the mistakes I'd made. They had no idea how closely I was observing their interactions with each other and their relationships with their kids. Through the witness of these families, I was drawn into a more authentic relationship with Christ.

Your marriage has the potential to be a powerful witness. One of the ways you can "fish" for men and women is through your restored marriage. Your children, family, friends, and other people in your sphere of influence are all impacted by your marriage story, and you're one of the determining factors as to whether that impact is positive or negative.

If you think people aren't watching you, think again. Being mindful to guard this gate means that at all times you're aware of what your marriage says about God to those around you. It's imperative to regularly reflect at the Fish Gate and ask, "What does our marriage say about God to those who are watching? How can we strengthen our witness for Christ through our marriage? In what ways can our family be an effective witness of God's love and desire to heal others?"

The Jeshanah Gate

> The Jeshanah Gate was repaired by Joiada son of Paseah and Meshullam son of Besodeiah. They laid its beams and put its doors with their bolts and bars in place. (Neh. 3:6)

The Jeshanah Gate is also referred to as the Old Gate. The application of this gate to marriage is best explained by the following verse from the book of Jeremiah: "This is what the LORD says: 'Stand at the crossroads and look; ask for the ancient paths, ask where the good way is, and walk in it, and you will find rest for your souls. But you said, "We will not walk in it"'" (Jer. 6:16).

Many marriage troubles occur because one or both spouses aren't focused on being a disciple of Christ as their first priority. The rising rate of divorce in the church is evidence of our need to get back to the basics of our Christian faith. Become an avid student of discipleship and marriage. Study the people whose relationship with God you admire. One of the best ways to do this is to ask others how they continue to grow in their relationships with Him, their spouses, and their children. Learn about the things others do to strengthen those relationships. Observe the interactions of couples or families you respect, and don't be afraid to ask them for help or advice.

Several of the ministries with whom we link arms are passionate about integrating marriage mentoring as an essential thread in the fabric of their churches. In Rutland, Vermont, for example, a team of pastors and their wives have banded together to implement a large-scale marriage mentoring program that spans multiple churches in their community.

Over the course of our remarriage, several mentor couples have provided us with wise counsel. The lessons we've learned from them have proven to be a resource on which we continually draw.

Most couples who have been through the fire will benefit more from having a mentor couple who has also been through the fire, sifted through the ashes, and risen together to heal. Can you think of a couple right now who might serve as your marriage mentors? Make a list of potential couples. Begin asking God for a mature couple who can be a regular resource and sounding board.

Mentors should be well grounded in the faith and have a strong individual relationship with God. Guarding this marriage gate means that you maintain a high regard for seeking counsel from those who have walked the narrow road of marriage before you.

The Valley Gate

> The Valley Gate was repaired by Hanun and the residents of Zanoah. They rebuilt it and put its doors and bolts and bars in place. (Neh. 3:13)

The Valley Gate leads us out of the city and down into the surrounding valley. This gate served as a perpetual reminder of one of the darkest times in Israel's history. During the period when the children of idolatrous Israelites were sacrificed to the pagan god Molech, they were brought through the Valley Gate to meet their death.[7]

No doubt you're well acquainted with the struggles inherent in a valley, or you wouldn't be reading this book. Spiritual valleys are those places you'll routinely travel through as long as you're living on this side of heaven. Sometimes our valleys, like those of the Israelites, are the result of disobedience and sin. Sometimes they're the result of someone else's poor choices. Regardless, valleys and suffering are an important part of the way God refines His children. But the Enemy wants to use the valley experience for a much different purpose: to distract you from your relationship with God and to divide your marriage. Standing guard at the Valley Gate means you take the necessary precautions to avoid falling prey to the doubt, discouragement, and disillusionment that loom in the valley when your eyes aren't fixed on God.

All the great saints of the faith knew seasons of suffering. Jesus plainly stated, "In this world you will have trouble. But take heart! I have overcome the world" (John 16:33). Reflecting at the Valley

Gate reminds you there will continue to be difficulties during your marriage journey. There will be times when you're both faced with a dip into the valley through an external circumstance such as the death of a loved one. Or you might experience a low in your lives due to an internal crisis such as unresolved feelings from your past or a setback during the restoration of your marriage. Ask God to use such circumstances to knit the two of you together more tightly.

In the valley, there are days when one of you will feel stronger than the other. During one season, you'll take care of your spouse; during another season, it will be your spouse's turn to tend to your needs. Lean into God through the entire experience, and pray that your hearts remain steadfast and faithful. Be intentional about asking God for ways to stick closely to one another despite the difficulties.

You may enter a valley at a different time than your spouse. When we moved from California to Florida in 2007, Clint was on top of the world. He longed to return to Florida where he'd lived prior to our remarriage, and he was excited about our new adventure. On the other hand, I wrestled with every aspect of our relocation. While Clint celebrated and embraced the change, I grieved over the loss of family, friends, and everything familiar. Although we both believed our move was orchestrated by God and we agreed on the move, still, having had my roots planted in the California soil for more than four decades, transplanting myself on the East Coast was one of the hardest things God has ever required of me.

Had Clint and I not been intentional about recognizing the differences in how we viewed and coped with the move, its impact on our marriage could have been devastating. Although Clint wasn't walking through the valley, he supported me and was patient. He gave me the freedom to do what I needed to in order to adjust. In a very real way, Clint stood guard at the Valley Gate on my behalf, observing and supporting my every step by walking beside me long after the boxes were unpacked. His faithfulness was a tangible demonstration of his love for me, even though he didn't completely understand my feelings.

Whether one or both of you is struggling, your journey requires humility before God and each other at all times. There are no short-cuts to the lessons God will teach you during tough times, but as you learn to be humble, the intimacy in your marriage will grow deeper.

The Dung Gate

> The Dung Gate was repaired by Malkijah son of Rekab, ruler of the district of Beth Hakkerem. He rebuilt it and put its doors with their bolts and bars in place. (Neh. 3:14)

Because of its name, you probably already have an idea of the Dung Gate's purpose. Located at the southwest angle of Mt. Zion, this gate was where the city's garbage and waste was taken out each evening. Daily disposal was critical to the health of the entire city.

You are wise to access the Dung Gate freely throughout the day. Subtle sins can quickly enter into the human heart, so you should symbolically guard this gate by giving God free reign to cleanse out the gunky buildup. "If we confess our sins, he is faithful and just and will forgive us our sins and purify us from all unrighteousness" (1 John 1:9). The foot of the cross is the only place to dispose of the waste our hearts collect every day.

One of the things that initially attracted me to Clint the second time around was how humbly he confessed the sins of his past. Later I discovered he had been attracted to me for the same reason. When God reconnected our lives, we were totally honest about the mistakes we'd made.

It is essential that you come before God in regular times of confession and forgiveness. The health of your marriage and family will quickly deteriorate if you neglect to honestly admit your shortcomings. It's never fun to admit that you're wrong, especially to your spouse. But complete honesty will never fail to enrich your marriage, no matter how difficult it may be to fess up.

The Fountain Gate

> The Fountain Gate was repaired by Shallun son of Kol-Hozeh, ruler of the district of Mizpah. He rebuilt it, roofing it over and putting its doors and bolts and bars in place. He also repaired the wall of the Pool of Siloam, by the King's Garden, as far as the steps going down from the City of David. (Neh. 3:15)

The Fountain Gate was most likely located on the southeastern wall of the city, next to the royal gardens of the king. Its location allowed for the irrigation of these gardens so the vineyards and plants would grow, fruits would ripen, and the gardens' full beauty could be displayed.

Symbolically, the Fountain Gate represents the filling of the Holy Spirit—a fountain that must continually flow in all our relationships. At the Feast of Tabernacles, Christ declared, "Whoever believes in me, as Scripture has said, rivers of living water will flow from within them" (John 7:38).

Each morning before I (Clint) begin reading my Bible, I specifically ask God to fill me with the Holy Spirit. I shudder to think about entering a day without drinking deeply of this life-giving fountain. Being filled is essential for the growth of my relationships with God and Penny.

In his book *Living in the Power of the Holy Spirit*, Charles Stanley writes, "Every day, ask the Holy Spirit to fill your life anew with His life-giving, joy producing, comforting, guiding, renewing presence. Every day, ask the Holy Spirit to fill you anew with His love, His peace, His truth. Every day, ask the Holy Spirit to fill you to overflowing with His compassion for others."[8]

Because of Christ's reconciling work on the cross, we have access to an unlimited source of power, wisdom, and love through the indwelling Holy Spirit. This is the same Spirit present in the apostles and prophets of long ago. Consider all the wonders and miracles performed through these men and women of the faith. The same powerful Holy Spirit lives in you if you've received Christ as your Savior.

The ongoing restoration of your marriage is fueled and fed by the Holy Spirit who is alive and working in your heart at every moment. Tap into His fountain. Guard this gate with passion. Ask the Holy Spirit to nudge you when you're walking a fine line or are tempted to repeat an old pattern in your marriage. Be zealous for more and more of the Holy Spirit and your marriage will overflow with the infinite attributes of God. Observe the working of the Holy Spirit in the lives of other believers. Ask God to increase both the measure and the manifestation of the Spirit in your life.

The Water Gate

> The temple servants living on the hill of Ophel made repairs up to a point opposite the Water Gate toward the east and the projecting tower. (Neh. 3:26)

In ancient times, only a portion of the city's water flowed into Jerusalem through a series of skillfully constructed aqueducts. The rest of the water got carried by hand through the Water Gate. This gate represents God's Word.

The book of Nehemiah mentions no repairs being made to the Water Gate. Of all ten gates, it was the only one that remained intact during the siege of Jerusalem. This speaks volumes about the holy and infallible nature of the Bible. Through God's perfect Word, we're cleansed from all our imperfections and presented blameless before Him.

> Wives, submit yourselves to your own husbands as you do to the Lord. For the husband is the head of the wife as Christ is the head of the church, his body, of which he is the Savior. Now as the church submits to Christ, so also wives should submit to their husbands in everything.
>
> Husbands, love your wives, just as Christ loved the church and gave himself up for her to make her holy, cleansing her by the washing with water through the word, and to present her to himself as a radiant church, without stain or wrinkle or any other blemish, but holy and blameless. (Eph. 5:22–27)

When our pastor finally found out our marriage was in crisis, he confronted us using this passage from Ephesians. At that point, I (Penny) already had one foot out the door and vehemently disagreed with anything and everything he said. I didn't understand the cyclical nature of the *mutual* submission described in this passage, mostly because I didn't want to. My heart was hard and cold. I was no longer guarding my time in the Word. Eventually I stopped reading it altogether. Closing my Bible, my heart, and my mind allowed the Enemy to ravage our marriage.

It's easy to let other things crowd out the time we should spend reading God's Word. So guard this gate by carving out your time with God as a nonnegotiable part of each day. Give someone permission to hold you accountable to your commitment of reading and applying the Scriptures to your life. Taking God at His word and getting the Bible into every crack and crevice of your heart is a lifelong pursuit worthy of your time and effort. Memorizing and meditating on Bible verses will keep your marriage in the center of God's will.

You will get out of God's Word what you put into it. The rewards and benefits far outweigh any costs.

The Horse Gate

> Above the Horse Gate, the priests made repairs, each in front of his own house. (Neh. 3:28)

Our next stop is the Horse Gate, located at the easternmost point in the wall. Scholars note that men rode horses only during times of war; thus, this gate was used by armies riding into battle. The Horse Gate speaks of the spiritual battles you have faced and will continue to face until you reach heaven.

> Finally, be strong in the Lord and in his mighty power. Put on the full armor of God, so that you can take your stand against the devil's schemes. For our struggle is not against flesh and blood, but against the rulers, against the authorities, against the powers of this dark world and against the spiritual forces of evil in the heavenly realms. Therefore put on the full armor of God, so that when the day of evil comes, you may be able to stand your ground, and after you have done everything, to stand. (Eph. 6:10–13)

We were pretty immature in our faith when we were married the first time. We had no idea how desperately the Enemy wanted to destroy our union. He went to great lengths to pull us apart, and his appetite to devour marriages is only gaining momentum in these latter days. Be absolutely certain of this: staying married means you'll have a fight on your hands. But remember, you are rising together to fight against the real Enemy, not against each another.

In their book *I Do, Again*, Jeff and Cheryl Scruggs identify the ways in which unprotected areas of their marriage gave Satan a foothold which eventually led to divorce. Cheryl writes, "If I'd at least acknowledged the possibility that I *could* have an affair—especially if I'd recognized my vulnerability—I could have protected myself."[9]

Standing guard at the Horse Gate means that, through prayer, you dress your marriage each day in the spiritual armor God has given you to wage war and remain protected. Not only must you clothe your marriage in God's spiritual armor but your children as well. Your children are the fruit of your marriage, and that fruit must have God's protection as it blossoms, grows, and ripens.

Visualize each part of God's armor being placed on your spouse from head to toe as you pray. To clothe your children in God's spiritual armor, you can do something similar at their bedsides or in the doorway of their bedrooms as they sleep.

The East Gate

> Next to them, Zadok son of Immer made repairs opposite his house. Next to him, Shemaiah son of Shekaniah, the guard at the East Gate, made repairs. Next to him, Hananiah son of Shelemiah, and Hanun, the sixth son of Zalaph, repaired another section. Next to them, Meshullam son of Berekiah made repairs opposite his living quarters. (Neh. 3:29–30)

Facing toward the rising sun, the East Gate was the first gate opened each morning. The watchmen who guarded this gate walked back and forth, making their rounds and keeping a keen eye on the city until the first light of day. In modern-day Jerusalem, the East Gate remains sealed. Some believe it represents the Golden Gate through which Christ will return. Other scholars say the East Gate is just a predecessor to the Golden Gate.

The East Gate symbolizes the ever-present hope we have in Christ. In the same manner that the watchmen and gatekeepers waited for the dawning of a new day, we keep watch and await the second coming of Jesus Christ "because of the tender mercy of our God, by which the rising sun will come to us from heaven to shine on those living in darkness and in the shadow of death, to guide our feet into the path of peace" (Luke 1:78–79).

Every month we receive countless calls and e-mails from abandoned spouses who have lost all hope that their marriage can be restored. While we offer them encouragement, we also know we cannot guarantee their spouse will return. What we can promise is the hope they have in a God who will never leave them hanging. "May the God of hope fill you with all joy and peace as you trust in him, so that you may overflow with hope by the power of the Holy Spirit" (Rom. 15:13).

Every year during our fall mission, we spend an evening with a group of men in New York who are all hoping for the reconciliation of their marriages. We're humbled as each guy shares his struggles and doubts, and we're reminded that a long time ago, another small group of godly men turned the world upside down because their hopes were set on Jesus Christ.

One of the group members, Dennis, who has become very dear to us, said it well: "Divorce is the pain that never goes away." Dennis is right. The pain of divorce never leaves. But neither does the hope he and the rest of these men are clinging to in Christ.

For Bill, another member of the group, that hope became reality. After the privilege of walking with him for seven years, we had the immense pleasure of attending the remarriage ceremony of Bill and his wife, Deb. They now attend our fall dinner meetings together. We pray that one day the table at which we meet will be surrounded by the rest of the men and their wives.

The East Gate symbolizes the new mercy you can claim as you arise each day. Someone once said, "Christ has turned every sunset into a new dawn." Until you reach heaven, you'll be in the process of restoring your marriage. You'll experience setbacks and make mistakes. But Christ offers His hope each morning.

The Inspection Gate

> Next to him, Malkijah, one of the goldsmiths, made repairs as far as the house of the temple servants and the merchants, opposite the Inspection Gate, and as far as the room above the corner. (Neh. 3:31)

At the conclusion of a battle, soldiers reentered the city through the Inspection Gate. Here the king would review and inspect his troops, carefully examining the state of his warriors. Strangers entering the city also had to stop at the Inspection Gate and register their presence; it was the ancient equivalent of obtaining a visa.

Applied to marriage, the Inspection Gate speaks of the account we as believers must give God regarding our deeds and words. "It is written: 'As surely as I live,' says the Lord, 'every knee will bow before me; every tongue will acknowledge God.' So then, each of us will give an account of ourselves to God" (Rom. 14:11–12).

As Christians, not only are we accountable to God, but we're also accountable to our spouse and other brothers and sisters in Christ. Accountability in these relationships simply means you intentionally ask a few people you trust to check up on your spiritual growth. For example, we both have prayer partners. These individuals have full access to our lives and permission to provide us with feedback and correction about our spiritual development and the status of our marriage. Being held accountable to the standards in God's Word and the standards in your marriage is essential to understanding God's plan and maintaining the courage to stick to it. Accountability/prayer partners will be discussed in greater detail in chapter 10.

Stopping at the Inspection Gate means sitting quietly before God on a regular basis and asking the Holy Spirit to examine your heart for impure motives, negative thoughts, and sins. One practical way of doing this is to picture your heart as a house with many rooms—bedroom, kitchen, living room, library, game room, attic, basement, etc. Ask the Holy Spirit to walk with you through each room and examine it for things that aren't pleasing to God. For example, in the game room, ask Him if all the ways you entertain yourself edify God, including the television shows and movies you watch and Internet sites you surf. In the basement, ask Him to inspect the things you may have unknowingly stored, such as bitterness or unforgiveness.

A powerful extension of this introspection is to engage in it with your spouse. This may take some practice, but a regular room-by-room inspection allows God to have full access to every part of your individual hearts and the heart of your marriage.

Coming Full Circle

> Between the room above the corner and the Sheep Gate the goldsmiths and merchants made repairs. (Neh. 3:32)

And so we arrive back where we started: at the Sheep Gate. What could be more appropriate? Coming back around to this gate symbolizes that Jesus Christ must be both the beginning and the end of every aspect of your marriage. As husbands and wives, everything you do and say must begin and end at the cross.

Pause and reflect at the Sheep Gate, asking God whether your behaviors, attitudes, actions, language, and so forth are completely encircled within His will at all times. Be still before Him. Shut out every other voice except God's. Allow the price He paid for your redemption to deeply penetrate your heart. Do you truly realize that you were the joy set before Christ when He endured the cross? Do you set His joy before you when serving your spouse and family?

Guarding the Gates of Your Marriage, Part 2 · *6:04 minutes*

Being a Marriage Gatekeeper

After the wall had been rebuilt and I had set the doors in place, the gatekeepers, the musicians and the Levites were appointed. I put in charge of Jerusalem my brother Hanani, along with Hananiah the commander of the citadel, because he was a man of integrity and feared God more than most people do. I said to them, "The gates of Jerusalem are not to be opened until the sun is hot. While the gatekeepers are still on duty, have them shut the doors and bar them. Also appoint residents of Jerusalem as guards, some at their posts and some near their own houses." (Neh. 7:1–3)

To conclude our tour, let's visually summarize the symbolism for marriage found at each of the ten gates.

The Sheep Gate: Your marriage must focus on God first. Regularly make sacrifices by putting God's desires and your spouse's needs above your own.

The Fish Gate: Be aware of the witness your marriage is to those around you.

The Jeshanah Gate: Regularly seek the wise counsel of marriage mentors and other support providers.

The Inspection Gate: You are accountable to God, your spouse, and others for every aspect of your spiritual and marital growth.

The Valley Gate: Remain united, supportive, and humble in seasons of suffering.

GUARDING YOUR MARRIAGE GATES

The East Gate: God offers new hope and mercy each day. Extend this same hope and mercy to your spouse.

The Dung Gate: Honestly confess your sins and mistakes to God and each other on a regular basis.

The Horse Gate: You are part of a larger spiritual battle and therefore must be shielded and armed at all times.

The Fountain Gate: Ask God to fill you with the Holy Spirit each day.

The Water Gate: Immerse yourself in God's Word daily and weekly as a couple.

Immediately after the gates were repaired and put back in place, Nehemiah set up a system of ongoing protection and defense over these vulnerable entry points. The gates of the city were shut and barred at the close of each day by the city's gatekeepers. Moreover, Nehemiah instructed the gatekeepers not to open the gates at the first light of day as had been their custom. Commentators reason that Nehemiah did this to prevent Jerusalem's enemies from launching a surprise attack at the gates during the early morning hours when people were still asleep.

Nehemiah chose reputable people to guard the city and keep watch over its gates. Posting people to stand guard near their homes demonstrated Nehemiah's knowledge of the human psyche: we are much more apt to guard well the territory that is dearest to our hearts.

Becoming a marriage gatekeeper is part of your responsibility to God and your spouse. It's imperative to keep careful watch over the health and balance in your relationship by regularly reflecting on and inspecting the areas of your marriage that each gate symbolizes. Not every gate in Jerusalem was in the same state of disrepair; some gates required more work than others. But because each served an important purpose, they had to be completely repaired and carefully guarded. There will be times where the same is true for your marriage.

Gary and Mona Shriver have lived through the pain of adultery and come out of it with great spiritual insight. Through their ministry, Hope & Healing, they now help couples recover from infidelity. The Shrivers share the following wisdom:

> Our culture cultivates male-female relationships. Whether or not trust has been betrayed in the past, intentionally setting up a few safeguards can go a long way toward protecting your marriage. Meeting alone with a person of the opposite sex can start out innocently, but we know how subtly a platonic relationship can turn into something neither person intended. Is it possible for men and women to be "just friends"? Of course. But an intimate friendship carries the risk of taking the road to something more. It's just the way we're wired.
>
> The choice we've each made is to avoid putting ourselves in situations with someone of the opposite sex where an emotionally or physically intimate relationship could occur. Now, we don't go around policing each other where these safeguards are concerned. It's our responsibility to stand by these choices and fess up if we fall short. Clearly communicating these safeguards to our close friends has been important too. Some people think we're a little paranoid about the agreements we've made. We tell them that if our decisions sound overly cautious, that's okay. Being considered silly or oversensitive is a price we're willing to pay

to protect our marriage. After all, we know the cost of not doing so.

Wise words from a couple who has been there.

Rely on the Holy Spirit to help you detect the places in your relationship that are vulnerable or in need of work. From time to time, you'll need to make repairs and ensure that all your marriage gates are set in place and functioning the way God intends.

Prayer to Guard Your Marriage

God, please protect the spiritual gates of our marriage. Help us remember that our relationship begins and ends with You. Remind us to not put anyone or anything in Your place. Show us new ways to follow Your example by sacrificing our desires and focusing on each other's needs before our own.

We want our marriage to reflect You to those around us. Give us opportunities to witness to others through our marriage and family. We admit that we don't have all the answers. Provide us with marriage mentors and other spiritually mature couples who can help us protect our relationship and keep it growing.

When trials come, show us how to walk through the valleys together. May we learn to follow Your example of humility in the face of suffering. Remind us to come to You daily and admit our sins. Grant us repentant hearts that seek and extend forgiveness. Fill us with an overflowing measure of Your Holy Spirit each day as we spend time in Your Word. Arm and equip us with everything we need to fight the battles we'll face. Clothe us in Your spiritual armor. Prevent the Enemy from discouraging or distracting us. Instead, let us fix our eyes on You as our hope.

Holy Spirit, hold us accountable to the things You require of us. Guard the gates of our marriage and help us keep watch over the things that matter most. In Jesus' name. Amen.

For a Marriage on the Mend

Making Connections

Illustrate a simple map of each of the ten gates of Jerusalem and what they represent in marriage (similar to the diagram found on page 175). Next to each gate, write one idea or tool you will implement to help guard what that gate symbolizes in your marriage.

Questions to Consider

1. Which spiritual gates in your marriage would you say are in the greatest need of repair?
2. Read Nehemiah 5–6. What kind of opposition does Nehemiah face and what do you notice about the ways he wards off his enemies?
3. How can you apply the symbolism of each of the ten gates to your relationship with your children?
4. As you look back over your marriage timeline, can you identify the places or times where certain gates were left unguarded?

Chapter 10

Retrofitting Your Relationship

Having lived in California most of our lives, the two of us are well acquainted with the earthquakes and aftershocks common there. When the Loma Prieta quake struck California in 1989, we'd been married just over a month. Many structures suffered major damage, and government agencies launched widespread efforts to inspect and retrofit unstable buildings, highways, and bridges. For those of you unfamiliar with the term, a *retrofit* allows for the modification of existing structures in order to make them more resistant to damage caused by seismic activity. If we had known how to retrofit our young marriage with tools such as the ones in this chapter, we would have had a better chance of surviving the major shake-ups we were about to encounter.

You never know when great difficulty may strike your marriage with earthquake-like intensity and threaten its sustainability. The focus of this chapter is to learn how to stabilize your marriage from the sudden jolts and aftershocks that occur as you continue your journey. Regularly guarding your marriage gates, inspecting the vulnerable places in your relationship where damage is likely to occur, and shoring up any instability will ensure that no matter what strikes, your marriage will remain standing long after the disaster has passed.

Till now, many of the tools we've given you have been *reactive*, to be used in the midst of or after a crisis. In this chapter, however, we'll provide you with several *proactive* measures so your relationship remains stable amid life's ups and downs. We'll also present several tools to help you work together as a team to defend and fortify your marriage. Utilizing a balance of reactive and proactive tools will make your marriage more resilient.

Through our continued study of Nehemiah, we'll also identify the types of opposition and trouble he faced and the wise strategies he deployed to meet his enemies head-on and defeat them. Keep in mind that your spouse is your ally, not your enemy. Uniting to face any and all opponents will make the difference between a weak marriage and a strong one.

Identifying Your Opponents and Their Tactics

As the wall around Jerusalem was being restored, Nehemiah encountered relentless opposition. Below are just some of his enemies' tactics to stop the process of restoration and rebuilding.

Anger, ridicule, and sarcasm:

> When Sanballat heard that we were rebuilding the wall, he became angry and was greatly incensed. He ridiculed the Jews, and in the presence of his associates and the army of Samaria, he said, "What are those feeble Jews doing? Will they restore their wall? Will they offer sacrifices? Will they finish in a day? Can they bring the stones back to life from those heaps of rubble—burned as they are?" (Neh. 4:1–2)

Scheming:

> Sanballat and Geshem sent me this message: "Come, let us meet together in one of the villages on the plain of Ono."
> But they were scheming to harm me. (Neh. 6:2)

Playing on inadequacies and weaknesses:
Tobiah the Ammonite, who was at his side, said, "What they are building—even a fox climbing up on it would break down their wall of stones!" (Neh. 4:3)

Fear and intimidation:
They were all trying to frighten us, thinking, "Their hands will get too weak for the work, and it will not be completed." (Neh. 6:9)

Slander:
He had been hired to intimidate me so that I would commit a sin by doing this, and then they would give me a bad name to discredit me. (Neh. 6:13)

Satan possessed a wide variety of weapons in his arsenal back then. He still does today. Many of his schemes are precisely and relentlessly targeted to destroy marriages and families. But we know that the ultimate victor in this battle has already been determined. Because of Christ's death and resurrection, you can trust God to use every bit of the opposition you encounter for a heavenly purpose. When your challenges are handled in a way that honors God, they will actually serve to retrofit your marriage.

Some of the opposition Nehemiah faced was internal and some of it was external. In the preceding Bible passages, his opposition was external: problems were coming at Nehemiah from sources outside the walls of the city. Sanballat, Geshem, and Tobiah were three troublemakers who relentlessly stirred up problems in an attempt to overthrow Nehemiah's efforts. Jerusalem had been lying in ruins for 150 years. Until Nehemiah arrived on the scene, all other attempts to rebuild the city had been aborted. Now Nehemiah's presence, power, and influence over the people posed a political threat that ruffled the feathers of Sanballat and his allies in a major way.

But other aspects of Nehemiah's opposition were internal. The workers who were supposed to be supporting the rebuilding efforts created some of Nehemiah's most monumental problems. Here are just two examples.

Discouragement and weariness among the laborers:
Meanwhile, the people in Judah said, "The strength of the laborers is giving out, and there is so much rubble that we cannot rebuild the wall." (Neh. 4:10)

Arguments and complaints against one another:
Now the men and their wives raised a great outcry against their fellow Jews. Some were saying, "We and our sons and daughters are numerous; in order for us to eat and stay alive, we must get grain."

Others were saying, "We are mortgaging our fields, our vineyards and our homes to get grain during the famine."

Still others were saying, "We have had to borrow money to pay the king's tax on our fields and vineyards." (Neh. 5:1–4)

Like Nehemiah, you've undoubtedly encountered both internal and external opposition, and you'll face them in the future as well. Internal opposition may be a spouse's life-threatening illness or a prodigal son or daughter who wanders from the family. External opposition might be a downturn in the economy, a meddling coworker, or an argument with a friend.

Regardless of whether his opponents came from inside or outside Jerusalem's walls, Nehemiah knew what he was dealing with at all times. He knew that the work he and his countrymen were engaged in would come under fire, and he planned accordingly. Someone once said, "A chain is only as strong as its weakest link." Nehemiah's actions prove that he understood this truth. He carefully organized the workers along the wall in order to ensure equal progress on all sides and to leave no part of the city defenseless.

So we rebuilt the wall till all of it reached half its height, for the people worked with all their heart. (Neh. 4:6)

Coming at Us from All Sides

Clint and I faced an example of internal opposition about a year after we remarried. I had accepted a promotion to a new administrative position in our school district. To celebrate, we decided to go waterskiing. During the last run of the day, I injured my back as the boat jerked me up out of the water. As a result of the injury, I had to leave my well-paying job and the school district I'd worked in for thirteen years.

Our whole lives were turned upside down. I struggled with not being able to work, do household chores, or accomplish much of anything. The accident significantly impacted our finances and our marriage. However, we made a conscious decision to ask God to use what had happened for good purposes. As difficult as the physical pain was (and still is) and the impact of my injury on our marriage, it was comforting and inspiring to see how God met us and led us at every turn.

Now, as we look back on all the incredible experiences that came as a result of God's sovereignty, we stand amazed. What could have taken our marriage down became the very thing that strengthened it.

At Clint's school, we faced an example of external opposition. As word of our unique reconciliation spread, we were asked to share our story on a Christian television program. During our interview, we candidly discussed the affair that ended our first marriage. A few days later, the producer of the segment placed the script from our story on the Internet. We thought little about it until months later, when one of Clint's middle school students came across our story and spread word of my affair around the entire school.

As a volunteer in Clint's classroom at the time, I'd gotten to know many of his students and happened to be present the day when the matter came to Clint's attention. A young man approached Clint after class and confessed that for several days, he'd been spreading the website and my affair around the whole school. He felt guilty for his actions and wanted to come clean.

"Mr. Bragg," the young man began, nervously scuffing his shoes against the gym floor, "I just wanted to tell you that I read all about you and your wife on the Internet and spread it around the whole school. I'm sorry."

Although we knew our story was becoming more public and we had agreed to expose our scars to help others, we were unprepared for the emotions that would accompany the exposure, especially at this level. What the student did hit me hard. I felt ashamed, and I hated to think that Clint could encounter problems at school because of my indiscretion years ago.

Clint could easily have gotten bitter toward me and become embarrassed by what was being spread. Instead, he responded to the young man with a dignity I'll never forget. He placed his hand on the student's shoulder, looked him squarely in the eyes, and said, "Son, thank you for telling me what you did. I accept your apology. My wife and I have nothing to hide."

Without our even having the time to figure out a response together, Clint united us as husband and wife. With that one simple response, we joined forces right in the middle of the unexpected external opposition.

Take a moment right now to think about a difficulty you're facing. Is it coming from inside your marriage or from an outside source? Sometimes half the battle is identifying the nature of the attack. Asking God to expose the truth of your circumstances allows you to clearly identify what you're dealing with. Sometimes after Clint and I have prayed, waited, and searched the Scriptures, God will reveal the nature of the opposition that we couldn't see at the onset.

Once you've accurately identified whether your opposition is internal or external, consciously decide to unite as a team and ask God for a plan to meet the specific opposition. Don't let down your defenses against Satan; be mindful that he doesn't want your marriage to make it. Agree to face your trials together, and hold each other accountable to your agreement. Leaving your mate stranded to do battle alone is *never* an option.

 Posting a Guard, for Women • *5:28 minutes*

 Posting a Guard, for Men • *7:31 minutes*

Posting a Guard

When Sanballat, Tobiah, the Arabs, the Ammonites and the people of Ashdod heard that the repairs to Jerusalem's walls had gone ahead and that the gaps were being closed, they were very angry. They all plotted together to come and fight against Jerusalem and stir up trouble against it. But we prayed to our God and posted a guard day and night to meet this threat. (Neh. 4:7–9)

Nehemiah's strategy for Jerusalem's defense included posting a guard who would keep a watchful eye out for enemies. It's wise to take a similar approach for the ongoing protection of your marriage. For our purposes, let's define a *guard* as "a person who watches out for the overall welfare of your marriage."

We have previously discussed the importance of having people in your lives to regularly provide you with wise counsel and hold you accountable to the standards in your marriage. Penny and I both have accountability/prayer partners who stand guard and keep watch over our relationship. We've given these individuals full permission to ask us tough questions, check on the progress of our marriage, and hold us accountable to our commitments.

I (Clint) prayed for months before God led me to my first prayer partner. Had the choice been mine, I'm sure I wouldn't have selected the man God chose for me. After getting to know Johnathan, however, I could see that God had designed a perfect fit for both of us. We are very different in our interests, but following the Lord and nurturing our relationships with our wives is at the core of our hearts. Over the years we've been prayer partners, we've gone through a lot together.

If you don't have an accountability partner, begin praying for one. God already has that person in mind for you. We've developed a checklist to help you find him or her.

- -
Qualities of an Accountability/Prayer Partner
- -

____ A mature, married Christian of the same gender (It is never appropriate to have an accountability partner of the opposite sex.)

____ Seeks God's will daily through prayer and the Word

____ Safe; someone with whom you can be honest and vulnerable

___ Willing to ask you difficult questions
___ Faithful and reliable
___ An advocate for your marriage
___ Will pray for you regularly
___ A trustworthy person who will maintain confidentiality
___ Willing to listen without judging

Many people drop their means of support and accountability once their marriage crisis has passed. That's a major mistake. You and your spouse should agree to maintain your accountability partners through every season, even when things are going smoothly. Your prayer partner will serve as an integral part of maintaining your focus on God first, then on your spouse. This person will provide you with perspective when you're selfish, wisdom when you're uncertain, hope when you're discouraged, and accountability when you're tempted.

Marv and Linda Rooks were married over twenty years when their marriage drifted into crisis. Their separation lasted three long years. Linda said, "At first, getting back together was scary because we were afraid of falling back into old habits. Thankfully, others came beside us to give us guidance, and we each met with people who kept us accountable. To this day, Marv continues to participate in a men's accountability group.

"These are changes we each needed to make to help heal our marriage for a lifetime. No matter how much time passes, we are aware of the need to keep growing together and to watch out for pitfalls that might cause a slide backward into bad habits."

Developing a Weekly Strategy

Nehemiah knew fully the importance of securing Jerusalem's gates against future attacks. No sooner was the reconstruction complete than he deployed a system for the city's ongoing defense

(Neh. 7:1–3). Some research indicates that he even fireproofed the gates with a bronze coating.

Part of our own ongoing proactive strategy to protect our marriage started six months before Penny and I remarried. Living on opposite coasts, we asked God for a way to protect what He was doing in our relationship. Then, every Sunday evening by phone, we took turns reading Scripture and discussing its application to our lives. We also shared prayer requests for the week ahead and closed our conversations in prayer together. One week Penny would lead our devotional time, and the next week it was my turn.

To this day, our habit of weekly devotions remains one of our foundational, proactive strategies to protect and defend our marriage. Every Sunday night we sit together in our living room for an hour. We read a passage of the Bible together and talk about its application for our lives. This is our time to connect in a meaningful way and make sure no problems are brewing between us. We also align our calendars for the coming week so we can guard against overcommitted schedules or breakdowns in communication, and prepare for the week ahead.

 Developing a Weekly Strategy · 9:27 minutes

If you've never had a couple's devotional time, here is a suggested outline. All you need is a Bible, a pencil, a notebook or journal, and open hearts.

Weekly Devotional Framework
- Take turns leading the devotional time so that only one spouse is responsible for preparing each week.

- Open each session in prayer, asking God to reveal Himself to you through His Word.
- The leader should select a passage of the Bible that's been meaningful during the week. Use a relatively short passage while you're getting started. The spouse who is leading should read the passage aloud while the other person follows along.
- Relate the selected passage to your lives through discussion. The person leading may also choose to share something meaningful from a daily devotional reader relating to the topic. The leader should briefly explain why this Scripture and devotional reading was chosen.
- Ask questions and give each other time to respond to what you've read. Don't criticize your spouse's responses; just listen. This is not a time to debate or argue opinions. It is a time to apply the Word to your lives.
- Lay out your calendars and discuss the week ahead. Put plans in place. Discuss any needs for support. Be certain you're not overcommitting yourselves.
- Take turns sharing prayer requests and pray together for the coming week. It's best if both spouses write down the requests in separate notebooks or journals. Share praises from the prior week as well. You'll be amazed at all the answers to prayer you see from week to week as you continue meeting.

The Israelites' approach isn't what you might call having a devotional time. But after they finished rebuilding Jerusalem's walls and settled in their towns, Nehemiah assembled them, and the Word of God was read in their midst. "[Ezra and the Levites] read from the Book of the Law of God, making it clear and giving the meaning so that the people understood what was being read" (Neh. 8:8).

The people responded to the Word by confessing their sins and praying for forgiveness. They reflected on the evil things they had done (as well as the sins of their ancestors) and recalled God's deliverance (Neh. 9). And they made a binding agreement to keep a covenant of obedience (v. 38).

Make your weekly time together a binding agreement and a top priority for the stabilization of your marriage and family. We understand that you're busy. Life's demands are intense. But that's why it's so critical to create a system to keep your relationship stable. With a fortified marriage, nothing can come between you as the pace of life quickens and the demands continue. So agree to come together for one hour once a week, and decide on a regular time and place to meet. Fifty-two hours a year is a small price to pay for something as priceless as your marriage.

Meet on the same day and time each week to establish a routine. Choose a quiet location free from distractions, and have an interruption plan should a problem arise; for example, what will you do if the phone rings or a child needs tending? Our family and friends have learned not to interrupt our devotional time unless there's an emergency.

It takes time to settle into a routine. For us, irritations between us often occurred just prior to our start time. At those times, the temptation to skip our meeting was immense. But we kept our commitment and prayed through our problems, even when it felt awkward or we didn't want to be together. God has never failed to answer even our feeblest of prayers offered in the midst of our struggles. Like ours, your own devotional time will seem easier some weeks than others. But eventually it will become a foundational part of your marriage that you look forward to each week.

If you have small children in the home, pray for a way to adapt your weekly devotional time to fit your family. Even young children can be taught that Mommy and Daddy need some time alone.

Several years ago, we were sent to Italy as marriage missionaries to a couple who had hit a severe crisis in their marriage. One of the tools we taught them was how to have a weekly devotional time. With four active children in the home, finding time alone together was challenging. But with persistence, the couple found a time that worked. In addition, they gathered their children for a separate family devotional each week and encouraged each child to take turns leading it.

We believe so passionately in the value of this tool that we self-published a year's worth of short devotionals in a book titled *Dance Lessons: A Weekly Devotional Guide for Couples*.[10] It follows the same format we have suggested in this chapter: a passage of Scripture, a short story, application, questions to consider, and a prayer for the week. The stories and questions contained in *Dance Lessons* were carefully designed to meet the challenges of restoring a marriage.

Be Equipped and Ready

Our move from California to Florida freed us from the threat of earthquakes, but now we faced the uncertainties of the inclement weather common to the East Coast. Having lived in Florida a few years prior to our reconciliation, Clint knew how important it was to properly hurricane-proof our home.

"If a hurricane hits, we need to be ready to board-up the windows," he explained. "If the windows blow out, the rest of the house won't stand against the storm. Every window needs to be completely covered."

Clint worked day and night for two straight weeks, drilling metal studs into the stucco around each window. Then he cut, fit, and labeled various pieces of plywood so they could be quickly affixed and bolted into place should a storm arise.

His efforts created quite a stir in the neighborhood. Nerves were rattled, and rumors circulated about why Clint was working so hard to prepare for something that might never happen. Many people stopped by to find out if he had some inside scoop on an impending hurricane. One day, after numerous neighbors had come over, Clint walked into the house and said, "Now I know how Noah felt!"

I laughed. "Yeah, and now I know how Noah's *wife* felt."

"I'm not doing anything to my house right now," one neighbor said. "I'll just deal with it if a hurricane hits." His words reflect the attitude many people have toward hurricanes—and toward their marriages. They don't understand why they should go to such great lengths to protect and stabilize their marriage. So expect some odd reactions to the precautions you take. Only when you've lost something precious do you truly understand what it means to have another chance. We know what it was like to lose eleven years of our marriage that we can never get back.

Nehemiah also knew better than to take the security of Jerusalem for granted or to get lax and let down his guard. He knew at exactly what points the city was still vulnerable. He knew what to do to protect Jerusalem, and he took appropriate precautions to ensure its safety. At times his protective measures may have seemed extreme.

Those who carried materials did their work with one hand and held a weapon in the other. (Neh. 4:17)

Neither I nor my brothers nor my men nor the guards with me took off our clothes; each had his weapon, even when he went for water. (Neh. 4:23)

Not only did Nehemiah and the workers along the wall remain perpetually armed and vigilant, but they also labored long and hard well past their usual quitting time. Nehemiah's tenacity and the protective measures carried out by the Jews are just two of the many applications we can examine and apply.

Take a moment to visualize those two verses in relation to your marriage. Picture yourselves with a tool in one hand and a weapon in the other. Commentator J. Vernon McGee explains that the tool—most likely a trowel—signifies that believers must build themselves up in their faith; it symbolizes the inner work we must allow God to do in our hearts at all times. The weapon—probably a sword—represents the sword of the Spirit, which is the Word.[11] We must wield God's Word as the sword that will never fail to protect and defend our marriage.

Nehemiah never dealt with his enemies in his own strength, and neither should you. For as many assaults as were launched at him, Nehemiah continued the work and called on God to take action on his behalf. He never wasted his energy launching a counterassault.

You too must continually rely on God to defend your marriage. But you don't have to do it alone. God is raising up restored couples and ministries to take back the territory of marriage and family all across our nation and abroad. Organizations such as the Association of Marriage and Family Ministries (AMFM) have united a mega-network of grassroots ministries whose sole purpose is to equip the local church with resources to fortify marriages and families. Many of these organizations specialize in particular areas of healing and recovery from issues such as infidelity or sexual addiction. AMFM realizes, as have we, that when a marriage is healthy, the family will be healthy. When the family is healthy, the church will be healthy, and a healthy church can change the world!

Become students of marriage. Make it a point to arm yourselves with useful strategies and tips such as those offered at marriage conferences, workshops, and retreats. Ask other couples for their recommendations, and commit to attending at least one seminar, retreat, or marriage conference each year.

Another simple strategy to strengthen your marriage is to interact with new people. About a year after we remarried, we joined a small group of couples at our church and gathered with them for weekly prayer, study, and fellowship. Through our meetings, we exchanged advice, books, resources, and ideas. Because the bond between us grew strong, we could also call one another in times of crisis. It was through this group that we found our prayer partners as well.

Keep at It

Take notice of Nehemiah's perseverance. He stuck to his vision and made progress even as trouble came at him in waves. His enemies' assaults were progressive in nature; when one tactic failed, they launched another more comprehensive attempt. At one point, Nehemiah's opponents were so desperate that they tried to intimidate him with false accusations which threatened to malign his reputation (Neh. 6:1–14). His response to their threats was a technique we should be swift to employ when the battle heats up.

> Sanballat and Geshem sent me this message: "Come, let us meet together in one of the villages on the plain of Ono."
>
> But they were scheming to harm me; so I sent messengers to them with this reply: "I am carrying on a great project and cannot go down. Why should the work stop while I leave it and go down to you?" Four times they sent me the same message, and each time I gave them the same answer. (Neh. 6:2–4)

In response to his enemies' repeated attempts to trap, intimidate, and distract him with lies and unfounded accusations, Nehemiah employed a broken-record technique. He prayed and prayed and prayed again. Four times his adversaries sent threatening messages, and four times he replied with the same answer. When these troublemakers continued to pester Nehemiah, he held fast to his convictions, prayed, and kept on working.

Despite all the forms of opposition his enemies threw at him, the restoration of Jerusalem progressed because Nehemiah had a variety of tools, both reactive and proactive, which he deployed at each sign of trouble. At this stage of your journey, we hope that you do too.

In the next chapter, we'll help you understand the importance of assessing the progress of your marriage with God's measuring stick in order to continue moving forward in the healing process.

Prayer for a Stable Marriage

God, as we face our problems, show us how to create strategies that strengthen and defend our marriage against all forms of internal and external opposition. Give us the strength to rise against the real Enemy and the wisdom to unite as one flesh. Even more than having You change our circumstances, it's our desire that You change our hearts. We ask You for a stable and resilient marriage, and we commit to never looking for a way out of our relationship, come what may.

Give us Your effective battle plan and grant us the strength to work together, facing every trial as a team. When You want us to be still because You will fight for us, help us heed Your advice. Provide us with resources, accountability, and wise counsel so that every aspect of our marriage is protected and pleasing to You. In Jesus' name. Amen.

For a Marriage on the Mend

Making Connections

If you don't have an accountability/prayer partner, pray about finding one. Ask God to lead you to the right person. Take a few moments to write down some of the qualities, common interests, and personality traits you hope this person will have, but be willing for God to surprise you. Be sure to review the checklist for choosing an accountability/prayer partner (pp. 186–87).

Questions to Consider

1. Think of at least one example of an internal conflict that you're presently facing, and one example of an external conflict. Which conflict is more difficult for you to deal with? Why?

2. In Nehemiah 8, Nehemiah assembled the people together in one place. What was the purpose of this assembly? What do you notice about the response and emotions of the people?

3. Of all the tools mentioned in this chapter, what are one or two ideas that you can immediately apply?

4. When do you find it most difficult to persevere in the restoration process?

5. What are the positive changes your spouse has made over the past several weeks despite opposition? Verbally affirm to your spouse the changes you've noticed.

6. Look over your marriage timeline again. Can you identify places where accountability/prayer partners would have provided you with wise counsel for big decisions and life events? Look at the blank section of the timeline (which represents what is to come) and discuss the ways you'll use some of the proactive strategies from this chapter to approach the future.

Chapter 11

Managing Your Margins

When we were married the first time, we had little understanding of how important it was to regularly and accurately assess progress in our relationship. We'd always been goal-oriented students and professionals, but it never dawned on either of us that we should have goals in our marriage, nor did we realize we should take time out to sit down and talk about our progress.

Before returning to California to remarry Penny, I had the opportunity to attend a seminar in which the speaker said he regularly escaped with his wife to discuss their marriage and family. He shared the ways they set goals together in various areas of their relationship to make sure it grew consistently. I was so intrigued that I told Penny all about it and asked her if she'd be open to implementing something like this. We had been doing a little of it during our weekly devotional time, but we didn't stop long enough to step back and gain a broader perspective.

Our discussions eventually gave birth to what we call a Mini Marriage Retreat. This chapter explains the basics of a Mini Marriage Retreat and provides you with some helpful how-to tips for implementing this idea in your marriage.

In order to continue growing, changing, and moving forward, you need to set and assess goals, discuss feelings, communicate struggles, and share dreams, all without the interruptions and busy-ness of everyday life. People set short-range and long-range goals to grow their businesses. Why not take the same approach to growing your marriage?

In order to accurately assess the progress of your restoration, you'll need two important things: time and tools. You must ask God to help you make the time, but all the tools you need are included in this chapter. We hope that by its end, you'll understand the inherent value of Mini Marriage Retreats and agree to make them a priority.

What Are Marriage Margins?

Chronic busyness plagues most marriages and families today. No room exists in people's daily schedules for reflection, solitude, assess-ment, prayer, quality conversation, and other things that require stillness and focus. These crucial means of nurturing relationships are devalued and displaced by an endless stream of activities.

Most families spend their days rushing from place to place. With technology and mass media feeding the insatiable thirst to be busy, more and more people lead a compulsive, activity-based existence. At one point, so did we. But the overly hectic lifestyle that characterized our first marriage eventually contributed to its demise. In contrast, learning to place adequate and appropriate *margins* (time and space intentionally set aside to assess growth) around your marriage will dramatically contribute to its health and well-being.

Overbooking your lives will make your marriage and family a much easier target for division. Building margins into your mar-riage means you give yourself permission to check out from the obligations and responsibilities of everyday living and check in with each other in the areas that matter most. Think of this intentional space around your marriage in the same way that margins surround a page of text. Margins exist to create and enhance a sense of order on a page so that meaning can be conveyed. Margins of time and space set around your marriage do the same thing.

Several times in the book of Nehemiah, we see that this faithful leader knew the value of stopping everything in order to pull God's people together. His reasons for doing so included garnering additional strength, engaging in corporate prayer, assessing progress, making changes, dealing with problems, taking oaths, forming alliances, creating covenants, fasting, confession, worship, and the reading of God's Word (Neh. 5:7, 12; 7:5; chapters 8–13). Nehemiah knew that maintaining reconciled relationships and focusing on what really mattered was extraordinarily close to God's heart. It still is.

Putting margins around your relationship will involve a deliberate, unwavering commitment to not let urgent matters keep you from regularly taking stock of your surroundings and making necessary changes. Look at it this way: you can't change a tire or get a tune-up unless you pull off the road and stop the car.

How God Measures Marriage

Mini Marriage Retreats are about assessing the growth (or lack thereof) in your relationship. But before we explain how these retreats work, it's essential to understand some truths about measuring your marriage the way God does.

Given that men and women have drastically different wiring, without God's perspective and measuring stick, it's impossible to accurately assess your marriage or agree on what it will take to keep moving forward.

Like many men, I (Clint) am a linear thinker. Processes, models, and structures are innate to how I function. But that's not at all how Penny operates. Creativity and thinking outside the box help her view, process, and respond to her surroundings. These differences, along with many others, make our marriage both an exciting adventure and a real challenge.

In our first marriage, we didn't understand that the different ways we were created should motivate us to follow hard after God's ways. Instead, we fought against each other to get our own way. Now we realize that letting God use our different temperaments to balance each other out draws us closer together. The result is that we become a complement to each other instead of a stumbling block.

As with Penny and me, your own personalities, genders, ages, backgrounds, qualities, and quirks can skew your perspectives on just about everything, including your marriage. You therefore need to seek God's vision and perspective in assessing your relationship rather than relying on your own. The way to develop accurate viewpoints and opinions is to measure your marriage according to God's yardstick. Let's explore three vital truths that can help you understand how God measures a marriage.

Upside Down

The first truth is that God's measuring stick is always inverted from that of the world.

Turn on your TV or computer and you'll quickly see the way the world measures a successful marriage: making money, raising smart kids, acquiring possessions, and enjoying great sex, to name a few. But the Bible consistently reveals a very different outlook. Consider the radical statements of Jesus, such as, "Blessed are the meek, for they will inherit the earth" (Matt. 5:5). "Whoever finds their life will lose it, and whoever loses their life for my sake will find it" (Matt. 10:39). "For it is the one who is least among you all who is the greatest" (Luke 9:48).

This inverted, upside-down sort of thinking is rampant throughout the Bible. We refer to it as God's Law of Inversion. It's from this principle that we derived the name for our nonprofit organization, Inverse Ministries.

Living contrary to how the world defines success, accomplishment, marriage, family, and so forth, is something to strive for every day. It may feel like an upstream swim, but we encourage you to stay committed to measuring every aspect of your lives the way God does. In the long run you will discover that the benefits and blessings outweigh the cost.

The Big Picture

The second truth about how God measures marriage is this: He has the bigger picture in full view—*always*. Your marriage is part of a much larger story. You see in part what He sees in whole.

Isaiah 55:8–9 states, "'For my thoughts are not your thoughts, neither are your ways my ways,' declares the LORD. 'As the heavens are higher than the earth, so are my ways higher than your ways and my thoughts than your thoughts.'" This passage is the plumb line we hold to in every area of our lives.

How would a shift in perspective change your marriage right now? In what ways has your perspective left you shortsighted? Regularly praying that God would expand your perspective on life and relationships is wise. Our capacity to consider more than our own viewpoint is severely limited. But the Holy Spirit can and will broaden your scope.

In Light of Eternity

Truth number three about the way God measures a marriage: the eternal perspective is always God's top priority.

In response to a wealthy young man who wanted to know what was lacking in his life and his relationship with God, Jesus gave an unpopular answer: "If you want to be perfect, go, sell your possessions and give to the poor, and you will have treasure in heaven. Then come, follow me" (Matt. 19:16–24). If you're familiar with this story, then you know that instead of following Jesus, the young man turned and walked away. You can almost hear him muttering and sulking under his breath, "If that's what it takes to follow You, I'll pass."

If Jesus came back to earth today, would the priorities in your marriage and family be in complete alignment with God's eternal priorities? In what ways are you and your spouse seeking God's heavenly kingdom over your earthly comfort? These questions merit sober consideration.

Once you begin to grasp the wisdom behind these three truths regarding how God measures marriage and apply them to your lives, your perception will be transformed and united under Him. There are few things more powerful than humbly submitting your differences, temperaments, strengths, innate qualities, and quirks under the authority of God and the power of the Holy Spirit. As this happens, you are wholly joined together in the spiritually intimate way God designed your marriage to function.

Managing Your Margins · *4:22 minutes*

Getting Away with God

Having examined how God measures marriage, let's look closely at how the Mini Marriage Retreat exemplifies these three truths, sets marriage margins, and helps you move your relationship closer toward God's grand design.

The concept behind the Mini Marriage Retreat is simple because, frankly, marriage is complicated enough. These retreats consist of a regular time set aside every three months for the purpose of measuring our marriage. Having logged more than forty-five of them as of this writing, we can attest that this simple structure has altered the course of our lives.

Once each quarter, we set aside everything except God and our marriage. E-mails and to-do lists are left behind. Cell phones are turned off.

Perhaps you're already thinking that getting away with your spouse even once a year would be a financial or logistical challenge, let alone three or four times a year. Please read this whole chapter, praying together and allowing God to help you tweak these retreats to fit your marriage, family, jobs, schedules, and budget. Engaging in these little getaways may not be easy, but had Penny and I instituted an idea like this the first time around, we might never have gone our separate ways.

Mini Marriage Retreats are prioritized on our calendars at the start of every year, before any other commitment. February, May, August, and November are the months that work best for our marriage and ministry. If the two of you can't do a retreat once each quarter, try at least twice a year as a starting point.

About three weeks before a retreat, we pray about the specific place God wants us to go. Choosing somewhere near home minimizes stress. We've been known to check into an inexpensive hotel only ten minutes away from our house. Over the years, we've kept a record of hotels close to our home, and we usually rotate through them unless God lets us know that He has something else in mind. We economize by using hotels that include a continental breakfast in their room package. The point is not where we go on these retreats, but what we do together.

If you have small children or cannot afford to get away, there are options. For instance, partner with another couple who is in the same boat. When it's time for your Mini Marriage Retreat, they can watch your children; then when it's time for their retreat, you do the same for them. Try swapping houses, condos, or apartments with people you trust. Perhaps the couple you partner with can watch your children in your home and you can use a guest room in their home as your retreat location, and vice versa. The point is that you're

completely alone and away from your house so you can avoid distractions. Discussing this idea with another interested couple may
also lend itself to other creative solutions to childcare issues, budget
shortfalls, and other challenges.

What a Mini Marriage Retreat Looks Like

We usually leave in the late afternoon of our first day. After check-
ing into the hotel, we freshen up and go out on a simple date. We
alternate planning these date nights so each of us has a chance to
decide what we'll do and where we'll go. During dinner, we talk over
some of our expectations for our time away. Our night out is to be a
time of enjoying each other's company without the stress of schedules, ministry, commitments, or problems.

The next morning, after breakfast and our individual quiet times,
we take a long walk. Then, with our Bibles, journals, and the list of
goals from our last Mini Marriage Retreat in hand, we find a quiet
place to meet, such as the hotel pool area. In the warmer months,
we can usually find a nearby park or picnic table. The hotel registrar
is usually helpful in pointing out possibilities in the area. When it's
too cold outside, we find a quiet conference room in the hotel or just
stay in our room.

We begin our discussion with prayer, asking God to guide us. We
open our journals and review the goals that were set during our previous Mini Marriage Retreat three months earlier. Reviewing our
past goals usually takes about ninety minutes. (Obviously, when you
take your very first Mini Marriage Retreat, you won't have a previous
list of goals to review.) We look at the things God helped us accomplish and discuss whether any unmet goals resulted from our own
neglect or because God led us in a different direction. The answer
to that question determines whether we carry any unachieved goals
over into the next quarter.

Regardless of the results, this time of reviewing and reflecting causes us to thank God for helping us work toward our goals. It also provides us with an opportunity to compliment each other about the growth we've seen in particular areas. Over time, we've realized that the processes God uses to help us reach our goals are often far more important than the achievements themselves. In order to maintain God's perspective on your marriage, you must always give ample consideration to the means as well as the end.

Husbands, you may not be as relationally gifted as your wives. For some men, just the thought of talking in-depth for ten minutes is a stretch. Give it time. When Penny and I first started taking Mini Marriage Retreats, the entire review and planning time lasted about thirty minutes, and then I was done. Penny wanted to discuss and develop our marriage standards, but I couldn't even go there.

Wives, please give your husbands a chance to ease into this process. Your conversations will become more fluid and natural. In time, you'll be amazed at the things God does through these retreats, and you'll look forward to the next one. Over the course of many retreats, our dialogue has expanded and deepened.

Once Penny and I have reviewed our goals from the prior quarter, we thank God for what was accomplished and pray for guidance as we plan ahead. Then we discuss and set goals for the quarter to come, breaking for lunch somewhere in the process.

During our first retreat, our goals consisted of committing to the date for our next retreat and setting four or five very simple goals. Keeping things simple at the start ensured our success and built up our confidence. Since then, our Mini Marriage Retreats have enriched our relationship so much that we often lose track of time. The retreats have been so valuable that about a year after we formed Inverse Ministries, we started using the same quarterly goal-setting system to measure our ministry and move it forward.

Once we finish determining our goals for the coming quarter, we offer them to God in prayer, always giving Him the permission to change, rearrange, remove, or replace what we've written down. Before we conclude our planning time, we also ask God for His clarity and direction regarding a date and location for our next Mini Marriage Retreat.

Because this second day's conversation is quite involved, we plan an evening that doesn't require a lot of deep thought or discussion. We may go to a movie or hang out in a local bookstore.

The next morning, we pack and head home. We pray God will help us to smoothly transition back to our routines and responsibilities and carry out the things He's planned for us. Having only a short drive home saves time as we return to our regular schedules.

The Seven Focus Areas

There are seven focus areas for the Mini Marriage Retreat. You may decide to make modifications to better fit your marriage and family. We've discovered, however, that these seven areas cover the basic functioning of most marriages.

Spiritual. This is the first category of the Mini Marriage Retreat and the most important. Goals in this area include anything related to your spiritual growth and development as individuals, as a couple, and as a family.

Relationships. This area includes your relationship and communication with each other, your children, extended family members, prayer partners, colleagues, and friends.

Health/Fitness. Goals in this category include regular exercise, monitoring your weight, making medical appointments, and anything else that keeps your body in good shape.

Professional. Goals that focus on your career or education belong in this category.

Financial. This area includes tithes and offerings, expenses, savings plans, taxes, and other financial matters.

Home. Repairs, furnishings, or renovations are discussed under this category.

Big Dreams and Possibilities. This area includes your individual and joint hopes and dreams.

Organize a Mini Marriage Retreat journal or notes in a way that works best for you. I (Penny) divide my journal pages into the seven focus areas and keep track of our individual goals as well as the goals for our marriage. The goals we agree upon in each area are listed accordingly. I like to use check marks to keep track of whether or not goals are accomplished.

- -

Sample of Penny's Mini Marriage Retreat Journal Page

- -

Spiritual Goals:

Penny:
> Memorize my life passage Isaiah 61:1–4
> Increase prayer time on Mondays and Fridays

Clint:
> Begin new study on life of Christ
> Memorize 1 John 1.

Our Marriage:
> Continue Sunday night devotionals and morning prayer together
> Find new home church in Florida
> Read one book together—Clint's turn to pick

There are several important aspects of each focus area that we'll clarify in the following pages to help you better understand the kinds of things we discuss. Our ideas are by no means exhaustive. You may want to expand on these areas. Adapt the focus areas and discussion items to fit your marriage and family, not the other way around. Start out slowly to ensure your success.

For your Mini Marriage Retreats to succeed at helping you grow and heal as a couple, the categories and goals must mean something to both of you. When you set goals, consider how much time will pass between the date you set them and when you'll revisit them during your next retreat. It's a good idea to write down the goals you agree on in your separate journals or notebooks and continue praying over them. That's what we do, and it has been exciting to watch God work in each area over time. Our journals have become a historical and spiritual record of all He has done in our marriage thus far.

Now that we've briefly explained the seven goal areas, let's spend some time unpacking each one in greater detail.

 Managing Your Margins—Spiritual Goals · *7:21 minutes*

Spiritual Goals

This category includes our spiritual goals as individuals, as a couple, and as a family. For example, I (Clint) may feel led to memorize some Scripture during the coming quarter. Penny knows I will recite the memorized verses to her during our next retreat. Things Penny might include as her spiritual goals could be spending more time in prayer and worship, or listening to a series of audio teachings on a book of the Bible.

One important aspect of this category is that when I share my spiritual goals with Penny, she listens, asks clarifying questions, and writes down my goals in her journal. I do the same when she shares her goals with me. That way, we hold each other accountable to our commitments and pray for each other's success. We're also careful not to condemn or criticize when goals aren't reached or when we set goals that are different from each other (which is often the case, given our personalities).

Our spiritual goals as a couple may be things like reading a book together during the next quarter, joining a small group study, or agreeing on a time for mutual fasting. For several months, we emphasized the work of the Holy Spirit in our lives and wanted to learn more about His power. So at one of our retreats, we agreed to read a book together on that topic.

A word of caution: make sure you don't exchange the spiritual disciplines that draw you closer to God for "doing things for God." God is far more interested in connecting with you than He is in what you do for Him.

This category pleases God and brings Him honor, and as you persist in applying it, He will continue to show you new ways to seek after His heart. God wants nothing more than for you, His children, to want more of Him.

 Managing Your Margins—Relationship Goals • *6:09 minutes*

Relationship Goals

In this category, we include our marriage and other relationships close to us. We discuss upcoming family get-togethers, birthdays, special events, and the ways we'll spend quality time with loved ones. Because my (Penny's) family is so large and there are many events, birthdays, and so forth, looking ahead and discussing these things in advance helps Clint to not feel overwhelmed.

We never want to take for granted the people God has entrusted to us. This category helps ensure that we don't forget what matters most. For example, during the first two years of our remarriage, Clint's grandmother had failing health prior to her death at age 101. So we agreed to travel to the assisted living center where she was staying and visit her regularly. While we were saddened when Oma passed away, we were glad we had prioritized quality time with her.

Your relationships with your children belong in this category. Maybe there is one child you need to spend more time with in the coming months. Or perhaps strained relationships between siblings require you to oversee some changes. One goal might be to have a family meeting at least twice during the coming quarter so you can all openly discuss issues and concerns. Again, make this category fit your family, not the other way around.

Our relationships with prayer partners and close friends also fit in this category, and relationships we're struggling with also come up for discussion.

Of course, our interactions as husband and wife are of the utmost importance. We talk about any difficulties we're having with each other and set appropriate goals for change. An example of such a goal might be to schedule a date night once a week or to be more intentional regarding affection.

Openly talking about sexual intimacy falls under this category. We never discussed sexual intimacy or physical needs when we were married the first time, but we do now. Of course, this isn't the only time we discuss the topic, but talking about these things outside the bedroom allows us to ask specific, thought-provoking questions and to listen to each other. For us, it would be a bit much to set goals about how many times a week we're going to have sex, but if you need to have that conversation because your schedules aren't in sync, then by all means, go for it.

What's important is that you openly and honestly discuss physical and emotional intimacy. This area is one of the greatest challenges in marriage, because our differences as men and women come into play here more than in other areas. Most men seek physical intimacy as a way to connect with their spouses, especially after a conflict. But women want emotional intimacy before they'll engage in physical contact. I (Penny) explain the difference by saying, "You have to touch my heart before you can touch my parts." Most women would agree.

The contrast in how men and women are wired in this area is one of the main reasons infidelity is on the rise. That was certainly the case for us. My affair during our first marriage was more about my unmet emotional needs and past wounds of violated intimacy than it was about physical satisfaction.

Prayerfully approach goal setting and deeper discussions about the topics in this category. God longs for your marriage to be intimate in *every* way. Because God is the only One who can meet all your needs, He can help you figure out what to change so that, despite your differences, both of you feel your needs are being met.

Managing Your Margins—Health/Fitness Goals · *5:40 minutes*

Health/Fitness Goals

The Bible says our body is God's dwelling place and a temple of the Holy Spirit (1 Cor. 3:16; 6:19; 2 Cor. 6:16). Therefore, it's essential to take good care of ourselves so that we can serve God well.

As we age, we're becoming increasingly aware of how important it is to ask for God's help to remain healthy and active. Perhaps one or both of us want to lose weight or increase our exercise during the coming quarter. Or maybe upcoming medical or dental appointments need to be scheduled. Talking about these things and deciding who will schedule them eliminates delaying routine appointments and exams.

We also discuss dietary concerns and the ways we sense God prompting us to make changes. For example, after uncomfortable physical symptoms led to medical exams and blood tests for Clint, we discovered that he needed to make dietary changes for the health of his heart. We talked at length about how to approach this. We decided to make changes to our eating habits as a team, even though the goal was really Clint's.

As in the other categories, some of our goals under health/fitness are individual and some are shared. The key is listening, supporting each other, and functioning as partners so we can work toward each other's successes as well as our own.

 Managing Your Margins—Professional Goals • *4:30 minutes*

Professional Goals

Goals and ambitions related to your career come under this focus area. This includes education, which can take many forms, from a master's degree program to a three-day seminar to a simple book that can help you improve in some aspect of your profession. For example, perhaps you want to take some classes that can move you toward your professional aspirations. When Clint moved back to California from Florida, he had to complete a series of classes to renew his teaching credential. He set a goal to take one class each quarter so he wouldn't procrastinate at getting his credential cleared or have to take all the classes at once.

Career-related goals might include putting together a personal résumé, investigating an opportunity for a promotion, or searching out a change in employment.

This category also helps maintain a healthy balance between home and career. Perhaps you'll be traveling for your job during the coming quarter. Many marriages fall by the wayside because out-of-control travel schedules require too much time away from the family. Discussing upcoming business trips, projects, timelines, and stressful seasons at work can be extremely helpful, especially if you have young children who need care and parenting.

The area of professional goals allows you to confront the issues that lead to today's epidemic divorce rate among couples with small children. Often the husband feels he is pulling all the weight of providing for his family, while the wife feels her husband has no clue to the demands she faces with the children. At the end of the workday, he's whipped and wants to be taken care of or just zone out for a while. But his wife is also exhausted from caring for the kids all day. When her husband gets home, she wants him to help with the children, or she wants the family to spend time together. If both parents are working outside the home, the problem expands. Both spouses are exhausted and money is tight.

Full-time parenting is a skilled profession that deserves the same respect and attentiveness as a career outside the home. Career goals need to be set for stay-at-home moms and dads with as much thoughtfulness as for any other profession.

In an effort to walk a mile in each other's shoes, some good friends of ours once switched places for a while. Annie taught high school and her husband, Rob, worked from home, took care of their son, and managed things around the house.

"When Rob and I traded places," Annie said, "we experienced the exact same feelings the other one had, and it really opened our eyes. It absolutely drove me nuts to come home and find the house a mess and Rob 'just sitting' in a chair, and it drove him crazy when I had no idea how often he washed yet another pile of dirty dishes or picked up Nate's belongings for the umpteenth time."

Raising children is particularly difficult when both parents work outside the home. But bear in mind, it's just for a season. The season will pass, and when it's over, what will the condition of your marriage be?

The point of bringing these scenarios onto your relational radar screen is not to solve them for you but to encourage you to regularly discuss your feelings, showing each other mutual compassion and support. If possible, go through a day in each other's shoes.

Don't set your marriage on the back burner amid the demands of careers and parenting. Instead, ask for help. Many have walked this road before you; tap into their wisdom. Most importantly, ask God for practical options before the divide between you grows so great that neither spouse has the desire or the energy to cross it.

 Managing Your Margins—Financial Goals · *6:14 minutes*

Financial Goals

What goals do you need to set when it comes to giving, expenses, debts, savings, investments, operating budgets, and other financial concerns? Do you need to get your taxes done in the coming quarter? Write it down and decide what needs to happen to prepare for the appointment. Perhaps you know that your property taxes will be due before your next retreat and it's a huge expense. Here is where to deal with it. Getting on the same page about upcoming expenses will keep you from being caught off-guard when the bills are due.

When we entered our remarriage, we made several goals that changed our financial state more than anything else we'd ever done. The changes that resulted because of them were so drastic and positive that we agreed to recommit to them each quarter.

Our first agreement is to tithe at least 10 percent of our income. No matter what the state of our finances, this commitment is nonnegotiable; if we view tithing as optional, we won't tithe. Sometimes, we test our comfort zones and our faith by giving additional offerings over and above our tithe. God out-gives us every time.

Our second ongoing goal is to pay off any credit card debts within the same month. We're committed to remaining debt-free. We also pray for the overall protection of everything God has entrusted to us, and we ask Him to safeguard our health, home, appliances, and vehicles from major or unexpected expenses.

Finally, in order to limit impulse purchases and other temptations to live beyond our means, we agree to what we call the "One Hundred Dollar Rule." If there is any single item we'd like to purchase that costs over a hundred dollars, it must be brought to the table and discussed at our next Mini Marriage Retreat. Gone are the days when one or the other of us would see some fancy tech gadget or piece of furniture and purchase it on the spot. This agreement has worked wonders for our financial well-being. It eliminates spontaneous buys that we can't afford; it ends conflicts over surprise purchases; and it has helped us pay off our debts and enjoy greater financial freedom.

Obviously, some expenses can't wait to be discussed at a retreat. Emergencies can arise that cost over a hundred dollars. However, making this rule our overarching policy helps us save a lot of money.

With large purchases, once we've prayed about them and arrived at a buying decision, we ask God to provide coupons, savings, or sales. Following our purchase, we place our hands on the item and ask God to bless and protect it so it can be used for years to come.

Once we were in the market for some outdoor furniture. Because the table and chairs we wanted were more than one hundred dollars, we discussed the purchase at one of our retreats, agreed upon a reasonable budget, and asked God for a good deal. Within a few weeks, we found the furniture on sale at a local retailer.

But upon arriving at the store and pricing everything out, we discovered that the total was slightly above the amount we'd budgeted. As we stood in line discussing our dilemma, an elderly gentleman walked up and asked, "Can you use this?" Imagine our astonishment when he handed us a coupon for a 20 percent discount. He hadn't heard any of our discussion; he was just passing some savings along. We could fill an entire chapter with similar stories!

Modifying these tips to fit your marriage will make a drastic impact on your overall financial health. Perhaps your rule needs to be reduced to fifty dollars or increased to a higher amount. Maybe you've incurred so much debt that you need a more aggressive approach to reducing it. Whatever the case, involve God. When you agree to tithe at least 10 percent of your income no matter what, God will provide (Mal. 3:10).

If you are in a financial crisis at this moment, Penny and I can relate. We entered our remarriage uncertain about how to merge our finances and handle our combined sinkhole of debt. Breaking our financial matters into smaller, three-month chunks made the process of paying off our debts more palatable and less overwhelming.

Financial concerns also became very intense after Penny's back injury when she was forced to leave her well-paying job as a school district administrator. Once her sick leave ran dry and her paychecks stopped, we had to make radical cuts in our budget. But while we were caught off-guard, God wasn't a bit surprised. He knew what was coming and prepared us.

Several months prior to the accident, when both of us were making a sizable income, we had discussed the possibility of buying a larger home that was closer to our school district. The long commute to school was horrible, and our present house was relatively small. But each time we looked into purchasing a new home, God closed the door. We felt confused but agreed that He was definitely leading us away from the purchase. We had no idea Penny would soon be off work and without a paycheck. Had we purchased a new home, we would have been strapped with a large mortgage payment that we never could have afforded on one salary.

This is just one example of the innumerable ways God has brought order to our finances. Never did we realize how setting goals in this category would so radically impact our lives and our desire to be in full-time ministry.

Managing Your Margins—Home Goals • *4:30 minutes*

Home Goals

Any improvements or projects that need to be completed around the house are placed in this category. If you don't own a home, adapt this focus area to fit your circumstances or living conditions. Your goals might include organizing closets or rooms. Perhaps you need to accomplish some deep cleaning. Maybe you hope to own a home, and your discussion and goals focus on that desire.

A common source of conflict between spouses is a husband whose wife nags him to do things around the house and a wife who feels frustrated because those things never get done. Penny and I have drastically different approaches to home chores and projects. Penny jumps on it; I take my time. After the honeymoon wore off of our remarriage, we started to have issues in this area. So we created a shared quarterly honey-do list and made an agreement to deal with the differences in our timelines. If a project is placed on that list, we discuss who will be primarily responsible for completing it.

What I love about this category is that Penny knows the projects I must complete, and I know I have three months to do so. She doesn't need to remind me. I admit that at first I took advantage of the ninety days and procrastinated until day eighty-nine. I didn't do it to irritate Penny, but I soon realized I was unnecessarily pushing her buttons by waiting until the last minute. Since then, I've changed my ways and learned the benefits of spacing my projects out over the three-month period.

 Managing Your Margins—Big Dreams and Possibilities · *5:11 minutes*

Big Dreams and Possibilities

It took several retreats for us to realize that we needed to regularly discuss our hopes, dreams, and possibilities, for both our individual lives and our marriage. That's when we added this category into our retreats. Once we did, we grew increasingly excited about dreaming together with God. In the past, we had both experienced the agony of watching our fledgling dreams get sabotaged by negative people, poor planning, or unfortunate circumstances.

So we're diligent to nurture each other's desires and to dream together as a couple.

It is an absolute joy to communicate our longings and explore great possibilities with our God of the impossible. This is an "all things considered" category. In sharing our deepest desires, we're careful to suspend judgment or criticism if we don't fully understand what's important to each other.

This category grants us the freedom to color far outside the lines and confines of "reasonable" thought. The book you're now holding is a result of our writing down our publishing dreams during many Mini Marriage Retreats. So are our 40-Day Marriage Mission Trips and our ministry to couples in crisis.

See page 220 for a Mini Marriage Retreat Goal Setting Worksheet with sample goals listed in each category.

Last-Minute Trip Tips

Here are a few other important tips before you try your first Mini Marriage Retreat. They can help you successfully implement this practice.

Agree to Disagree: Despite all the tools in our marriage tool belt, there have been times when we weren't in total agreement about a particular area of our marriage. You'll experience this as well. Expect to disagree, but take your differences of opinion to God on the spot. This bears repeating: ask God for the changes He wants to make in *your* heart and leave your spouse to Him. Remember to combine prayer with the Gradients of Agreement diagram in chapter 8.

Divide and Conquer: Taking care of the logistics for a Mini Marriage Retreat shouldn't fall on one spouse. This is a shared experience with shared responsibilities.

Mini Marriage Retreat Goal-Setting Worksheet

Focus Area #1: **Spiritual**	Individual—memorize 1–2 verses of Scripture Together—meet one hour on Sunday nights for devotional time Family—share blessings and prayer requests more intentionally Church—engage in church makeover service project
Focus Area #2: **Relationships**	Together—plan date nights twice a month (alternate who plans the date) Family—invite extended family over for dinner Friends—write one personal note to our prayer partners
Focus Area #3: **Health/ Fitness**	Self—increase walking by a half-mile each day Spouse—integrate free-weight routine twice weekly Both—get complete physical exams from primary doctor
Focus Area #4: **Professional**	Self—attend training for videography Spouse—complete one professional growth unit toward credential Kids—help with school loan application
Focus Area #5: **Financial**	Give 15 percent tithe for at least two months Reduce monthly expenses by at least 10 percent Open Roth IRA for both of us
Focus Area #6: **Home**	Weed and replant front flower bed Repair back gate and section of fence Pray for protection from major expenses
Focus Area #7: **Big Dreams and Possibilities**	Self—publish a book about our marriage journey Spouse—attend videography school Together—travel to Israel for a study tour

Know Before You Go • 4:47 *minutes*

Know Before You Go: Here is a short list to help you prepare for retreats with the minimum amount of stress and/or obstacles.
· Pray before, during, and after your Mini Marriage Retreat.
· Ask God to help you select a location. Decide which of you will be responsible for making arrangements and securing reservations.
· Determine your budget ahead of time.
· Map out driving directions to prevent getting lost or wasting time.
· Familiarize yourselves with what's nearby (restaurants, movie theaters, mini-marts) and what isn't. Plan accordingly.
· Pack snacks and munchies to save money.
· Discuss your expectations for the retreat beforehand.
· Discuss timelines (when you will leave, return, pick up the kids, etc.).
· Secure child and pet care. (To save money, consider house swaps, child swaps, and pet swaps with other couples who also want to take a Mini Marriage Retreat.)
· Discuss possible things to do together during the retreat.
· Leave your excess baggage at home (work, e-mail, etc.).

Heads Up: It took us a retreat or two to realize the Enemy directly opposed our getaways. Stay alert to Satan's desire to divide you and thwart your progress. Keep watch over each other as well.

Get on the Same Page: Retreats are a great opportunity to choose a new book to read together. Approach this idea as a learning process. It will take you time to agree on preferred genres. Ask for God's help in choosing books, and take turns making selections. You'll do well to select shorter books at first. In time, you'll learn which kinds of books work for both of you. Ask your friends, pastors, or local Christian bookstore staff for their recommendations as well. Below are some discussion prompts to get you on the same page with your spouse through reading and discussing Christian literature.

Getting on the Same Page · *5:36 minutes*

Discussion Prompts for Reading Books Together

I can relate to this chapter because . . .
One thing that spoke to my heart is . . .
What do you think about . . .
My favorite part of this book so far has been . . .
One thing I want to apply from this chapter is . . .
One of the things I appreciate about this author is . . .
I want to know more about . . .
I can identify with the author when he/she said . . .
I would recommend this book to _____ because . . .
A passage of Scripture that relates to this chapter is . . .
I'm struggling with what we are reading because . . .

Talk to Other Couples

Is a Mini Marriage Retreat the only way to assess your marriage or put margins of time and space around your relationship? No.

You might come up with your own system or use parts of ours and combine it with other ideas you come across. Talk to other couples about how they assess their marriage and put margins in their lives. Spend time exchanging ideas. Remember, the key is to *regularly* set aside *quality* time for the purpose of assessing your relationship and its progression. Perhaps you can partner with another couple and hold each other accountable to taking at least two Mini Marriage Retreats this year.

During one of our 40-Day Marriage Mission Trips, we met Steve and Shay—an amazing couple who were willing to take in two marriage missionaries whom they had never met until the day we stood on their front porch. Little did we realize how God would use that first meeting as the catalyst for many discussions and rich fellowship for years to come. Over time, Steve and Shay disclosed the struggles that almost ended their marriage.

"Eight years into our marriage, we bottomed out. We had two children under the age of three, and Steve was working out of town a lot—sometimes only returning home every other weekend. Not only were we facing these challenges, but we'd overcommitted ourselves by leading Bible studies, teaching Sunday school, and being regularly involved in more social activities than we could manage. On the outside, we looked like the perfect Christian couple, but on the inside, the busyness and sinfulness of life was more than our young marriage could handle."

"Time pressures, emotional distance, and selfishness were driving us into real trouble," admitted Steve. "Before long there was more bad than good in our marriage. We loved each other and really didn't want a divorce, but we were without hope that things could really change. Through some loving mentors, we realized we couldn't make our marriage work without the power of God's love in it. They had us rewrite our marriage vows and commitments along with other practical things. For example, we promised to put

the kids down at a consistent time each night and to use that time
to talk."

"We've now been married over forty years—most of them great,"
Shay said. "However, our marriage is not simply an accomplishment. It's a process that takes effort every day, forever. From time to
time we still have to regroup because the demands of life threaten to
crowd in on us. We've finally learned that busyness is not from God,
but it's so easy to get caught up in its trap."

Steve chimed in. "Thankfully, we have several strategies to keep
our focus on God and be intentional about having time together.
We pray and talk every day—out loud and eye-to-eye. Actually, we
talk 'feet-to-feet' from both ends of the couch. We call this 'talk
time,' and it's something that can be requested by either of us.
When a request is made, we set a time and meet on the couch. In
addition, we're both willing to wave the flag that says we need time
together, and we have several phrases that signal distress, such as, 'I
need some of your time,' or, 'My bucket is empty.' A healthy marriage requires discipline and commitment, but with those things
comes great rewards in closeness. However you do it, marriage is all
about intentionally making quality time to focus together on your
relationship."

 Managing Your Margins Next Steps • 5:03 *minutes*

Start Small; Pray Big

Take the suggestions in this chapter in bite-size pieces. If you
try to implement everything at once, you'll get overwhelmed. Allow
God to measure your marriage His way and embrace whatever

means He uses to do so. He's planned out your course and has been longing for you to accept His invitation to an incredible experience. A large portion of your journey is taken through prayer. Our hope is that through each of your Mini Marriage Retreats, you'll experience deeper intimacy in your marriage and your individual relationships with God. The moment you truly begin to tap into God's plan, perspective, and purpose for your marriage, you're in for the ride of your life. So fasten your seatbelts and hang on!

Prayer to Manage Your Margins

God, You know the demanding pace of our lives. We need Your help to place margins of time and space around our marriage and family. Show us how to value stillness, reflection, conversation, and assessment. We acknowledge how important it is to measure our marriage the way You do, not as the world does. Make us sensitive to the passages in Your Word that demonstrate your Law of Inversion so we learn Your ways. We ask for Your eternal priorities to become ours. Broaden our perspective so that we can see more than just our own needs, wants, and desires. Help us implement times of setting and assessing goals for all the important parts of our relationship. Bring other couples into our lives who share this same desire, and help us partner with them. We open our hearts and minds to the ways You want to change our lives. In Jesus' name we pray. Amen.

For a Marriage on the Mend

Making Connections

As a practice run, take some time to set one sample goal together in each of the seven focus areas. Look over your calendar and budget to discuss how feasible Mini Marriage Retreats would be. If possible, set a date for your first one.

Questions to Consider

Read Nehemiah 12:27–47 and Nehemiah 13 before answering the
following questions.

1. After the dedication of Jerusalem's walls, why do you think
   Nehemiah returned to his service as the king's cupbearer
   instead of staying in Jerusalem as governor?
2. What happened when Nehemiah later returned to Jerusalem
   to check on the people? How would you have felt if you were in
   his shoes, and how would you have reacted?
3. What are some of your initial thoughts and reactions regarding the Mini Marriage Retreat?
4. What is a feasible plan for the two of you to implement something like a Mini Marriage Retreat? Is it conceivable to get
   away four times a year? Two? What are some obstacles to consider ahead of time?
5. Look back over your marriage timeline and identify the times
   when you took on too many responsibilities. How did that
   busy season impact your relationship?

Chapter 12

Traveling into New Territories

Traveling into New Territories · *4:56 minutes*

Of all the content we could have written in this closing chapter, our choice of what made the final cut was a no-brainer. However, there was no shortage of options vying for control of the keyboard. For example, given that we've spent eleven chapters avidly following on the heels of the Israelites as they rebuilt Jerusalem's wall, one option was to direct your attention to the project's astounding completion.

So the wall was completed on the twenty-fifth of Elul, in fifty-two days. (Neh. 6:15)

Inconceivable! The wall around a city that had lain in ruins for almost 150 years was repaired in less than two months. In today's society, driven as it is by swift and favorable results, surely this feat merits our admiration—as does the progress you've made in restoring your marriage. If you've faithfully implemented the tools we've suggested throughout this book, then we're certain you've made significant growth and we commend you.

Unlike Jerusalem's rebuilding, though, the restoration of your marriage will never end. Nehemiah and his hearty band of laborers eventually hung up their trowels and tool belts. But if you follow suit, you'll find yourselves in a heap of trouble in nothing flat. Many couples make a grave error in assuming that once the disaster has passed and sufficient progress has been made, they can stop applying the strategies so crucial to their restoration. They thus sever the very things that knit them back together, and things once again begin to unravel. Please, don't follow their example.

Mending a marriage is not a one-time event. It is an ongoing process that you must cultivate every day for the rest of your lives. Reconciliation must become an integral thread in the fabric of your marriage, hemming in your identity as a couple—your "us" as husband and wife. There's no point at which you'll finish restoring your relationship. To this day, Clint and I still have things to work through. Some of this work is just part of the process God is using to transform us, and some of it comes from the poor choices we made in the past. Until the day we arrive at heaven's gates, God will not be finished restoring our marriage, and as long as you are on this side of heaven, He won't be done with yours either. Whenever you look around and think you've arrived, stop and take another look.

We encourage you to reread the advice from the couples who have contributed their wisdom in various places throughout this book. Like you, somewhere in the midst of their crises, they decided to fight for their marriage. And through a lot of hard work and God's grace, their marriages are making it. Keep your own tool belt strapped on tightly at all times. You're going to need it.

Another option that jockeys for a prime position in this final chapter is the rich symbolism and historical significance of the ceremonies recorded in the latter half of Nehemiah, and their application to your marriage. Not only did Nehemiah carry out the registry of all the exiles who returned to Jerusalem, but he also called for a lavish and unprecedented time of confession and celebration. No sooner were the doors set into the gates than Nehemiah appointed guards, gatekeepers, ministers, and singers to their respective places (Neh. 7:1). In Nehemiah chapters 8–12, we find the details of an elaborate gathering that included the reading of God's Word, corporate confession and worship, and a public declaration of faith. Integrated into all of this was the customary Jewish celebration of the Feast of Tabernacles, which commemorated God's protection during the desert wanderings of Israel's forefathers as they journeyed from Egypt to Canaan (Exod. 23). Just look at the way Nehemiah describes this grand affair:

> From the days of Joshua son of Nun until that day, the Israelites had not celebrated it like this. And their joy was very great. (Neh. 8:17)

It's hard to imagine what it must have been like to participate in festivities of this magnitude, whose latent energy had been building for centuries. When all was said and done, their celebration culminated in the dedication of Jerusalem's walls (Neh. 12).

As with the Israelites, the progress you've made in mending your marriage is cause for much rejoicing. Never hesitate to recall, acknowledge, and give thanks for what God has done. We commend you for courageously treading this challenging terrain. You've taken major strides on the road to healing and wholeness. Your family's spiritual legacy has been altered forever because of your journey. Retelling and reflecting on what has transpired in your relationship is healthy, appropriate, and biblical. So pause often, ponder the ripple effect of your choice to save your marriage, and linger there for a long, long time.

It's tempting to spend our words inspiring you with the unfathomable ways God will use your testimony of reconciliation to help
others. Because the truth is, the people best equipped to work with
couples in crisis aren't those with "perfect" marriages but other couples who have themselves been through the fire and risen from the
ash heap with their hearts in full-blown pursuit of God—husbands
and wives who are willing to show their scars and point people to
the One who healed them.

But whether God will lead you into marriage ministry is not our
call to make. It's His, and we'd be foolish to intervene on such sacred
turf. It's enough to say that God is passionate about using the power
of testimony to overcome every enemy (Rev. 12:11). We're absolutely
undone by how He works through our pain for His redemptive
purposes; however, we also know there are dangers inherent in any
attempt to foretell your future. Yet if God does choose to use the
story of your saved marriage to serve others, we'll be the first to
wholeheartedly welcome you to the front lines of this noble work.
We need more hands! We'll be knee-deep in the rebuilding effort
right beside you to snatch back every inch of territory the Enemy has
stolen. Oh, that our world may be touched by the restorative reach
of a loving God!

The topics we've described would all make a viable conclusion.
But early in the conception of this book, we knew that anything less
than making one last push to launch you even deeper into your relationship with God would be grossly negligent on our part. We've
entitled this chapter "Traveling into New Territories" in the hope of
enticing you into unprecedented intimacy with God. We long most
earnestly for you to give God greater access to your lives than you've
ever given Him before. It's the grand landscape of your soul that He
longs to fully occupy—and when God moves in, He likes plenty of
leg room.

Prone to Wander

No sooner had Nehemiah left Jerusalem and returned to the king's service than everything he'd labored for began to unravel. It didn't take long for the people to become careless and apathetic toward their pursuit of God.

> Before this, Eliashib the priest had been put in charge of the storerooms of the house of our God. He was closely associated with Tobiah, and he had provided him with a large room formerly used to store the grain offerings and incense and temple articles, and also the tithes of grain, new wine and olive oil prescribed for the Levites, musicians and gatekeepers, as well as the contributions for the priests.
>
> But while all this was going on, I was not in Jerusalem, for in the thirty-second year of Artaxerxes king of Babylon I had returned to the king. Some time later I asked his permission and came back to Jerusalem. Here I learned about the evil thing Eliashib had done in providing Tobiah a room in the courts of the house of God. I was greatly displeased and threw all Tobiah's household goods out of the room. I gave orders to purify the rooms, and then I put back into them the equipment of the house of God, with the grain offerings and the incense.
>
> I also learned that the portions assigned to the Levites had not been given to them, and that all the Levites and musicians responsible for the service had gone back to their own fields. So I rebuked the officials and asked them, "Why is the house of God neglected?" (Neh. 13:4–11)

Despite Nehemiah's exceptional leadership and the great lengths to which he had worked to ensure the protection of Jerusalem;

despite all the ceaseless striving, hard labor, new reforms, and a binding agreement to uphold the law that was sealed in public (Neh. 9:38); despite all these things, the Israelites made one critical error: they denied God full access to their hearts. Regardless of their humble confessions and an absolute resolve to remain faithful, they flaked out.

Eliashib was one of the priests mentioned as a laborer at the Sheep Gate (Neh. 3:1). How ironic. No sooner did Nehemiah return to his service as the king's cupbearer than Eliashib gave one of Israel's archenemies access to a sacred room in the courts of God's temple.

"We will not neglect the house of our God," said the Israelites (Neh. 10:39). If only they had lived out their words instead of merely reciting them. The people accomplished an amazing feat in restoring the ruins of the city, but they failed miserably in reforming their own hearts.

The Israelites missed a major revelation: the wall around Jerusalem was a symbol of the nation itself. Just as other nations had laid siege to the holy city, battered down her walls, burned her gates, and invaded her territory, disobedience had done the same thing to the people. The hearts of God's chosen people had been invaded by the things of the world, rendering them defenseless.

Consider this truth for a moment; let it sink in bone marrow deep. Just as Nehemiah longed to repair Jerusalem's walls, God longed to revive His people, shore up their foundation, rebuild their broken places, and restore them to an even greater glory than in days of old. The walls of Jerusalem, which had remained in disrepair so many years, symbolized the disobedient state of the nation. But the people never made that connection; this critical truth went right over their heads.

Sin had ravaged their hearts for generations, and their relationship with God lay crumbled. Only ruins remained. However, God had a plan and a Person to restore the nation—and His people.

Staying True to Form

> This is what he showed me: The Lord was standing by a wall
> that had been built true to plumb, with a plumb line in his
> hand. And the LORD asked me, "What do you see, Amos?"
> "A plumb line," I replied.
> Then the Lord said, "Look, I am setting a plumb line among
> my people Israel; I will spare them no longer." (Amos 7:7–8)

A plumb line is a simple tool consisting of a cord with a stone or weight suspended at one end, pointing the cord directly toward the earth's center of gravity. A plumb line is used to ensure that vertical structures are perfectly upright. Biblical references to a plumb line almost always symbolized how uprightly God's people were living according to His Word. A plumb line signified the standard by which God would judge His people, and the mention of it let them know that enough was enough: judgment was coming. While God's people were originally created true to plumb, they did not remain upright when tests and trials arose. A righteous and just God could not idly sit by and allow their disobedience to continue.

We don't see a plumb line mentioned in the book of Nehemiah, but such a tool would have been freely used in the reconstruction process. As the walls went up, it was important to make sure they were true to plumb. Ironically, while the walls remained straight, the hearts of the people rapidly leaned toward sin.

We'd do well to learn from the Israelites' mistakes, but a glance at our nation today shows that many people are repeating them instead. The human heart, so precious to God, gets treated like nothing more than a cheap bargaining chip in the quest for the things of this world. As a nation, we're quick to profane what is sacred. Between around-the-clock assaults from mass media, technological advances, and Internet offerings at our fingertips, the pursuit of earthly pleasures over kingdom purposes knocks incessantly at our heart's door. And despite the high morals to which we hold as Christians, each of us is just a click away from desecrating God's dwelling place.

So if you aren't spending what fleeting time you have left on earth intentionally and reverently seeking God, then somewhere down the road you'll find yourself in crisis all over again. You'll close the last page of this book, and it and your marriage will sit on a shelf collecting dust—because if you don't seek to fill every square inch of your heart with more of God, it *will* be filled with other things.

Like the ancient Israelites, we need a plumb line, and we have one in Jesus Christ. Through His death, Jesus humbly holds the bar by which we must measure our lives. In many respects, Nehemiah and many other leaders, prophets, saints, apostles, martyrs, and disciples were forerunners of the Plumb Line who was to come. Like Christ, these forerunners chose to exercise humility over power and to forgive instead of fight. Like Christ, their attitudes and actions went against the grain of the world. The manner by which they stayed true to plumb was so unfathomable that, more often than not, they were persecuted for rubbing the world the wrong way, especially when it came to relationships. Take a look at just a few examples of these courageous forerunners in God's Word:

- Abraham bound his son and his hopes to the altar of sacrifice.
- David had Saul at the end of his spear, yet refused to take revenge.
- Ruth remained by her mother-in-law's side instead of returning to her homeland.
- Hannah gave birth after years of barrenness and then gave her son back to God.

- Joseph forgave his jealous brothers despite their attempt to kill him.
- Esther risked her life to save her people from annihilation.
- Hosea reconciled with his wife even though she'd sold herself for sex.

If you took the time to trace the favorable fallout from those seven people, you'd discover that they drastically altered the course of human history. Many more people, past and present, belong on that list as well. All of these heroes have this in common: they learned to live under God's Law of Inversion in every aspect of their lives, especially where relationships were concerned. They understood that in order to be great, they must become the least, and that to possess true love, they must give love away. As extraordinary as the way these people lived plumb to God's principles, is how sheer love and obedience guided their choices.

Our beloved Nehemiah made those same kinds of inverted choices. Let's extract a few final principles from our favorite leader—truths so subtle and countercultural that they're easily overlooked and tempting to avoid. Not until the two of us engaged in a much more active and intentional approach to our own relationships with God did we began to scratch past the surface of the three empowering Plumb Line Principles we're about to unpack. Grasping these truths will hold you and your marriage true to God's original design.

Unlike the previous lessons we've drawn from Nehemiah, these three principles are revealed not through what Nehemiah did but through what he *didn't* do.

Plumb Line Principle 1: Less Is More

Throughout his life, Nehemiah never chose opportunism over service. His priority was to be a humble servant, first to God and then to his fellow man. He was a servant leader, and he lived out that characteristic in various forms. For example, unlike other political figures, instead of demanding the food rightfully allotted to him, he made sure that others had what they needed. Nehemiah wasn't worried about feeding his stomach or his ego.

During his tenure as governor, he also chose not to acquire any land. A servant's heart for God and His people was the gauge by which Nehemiah set his priorities. Any possessions he may have acquired were never hoarded. Instead, Nehemiah regularly entertained a variety of guests at his own expense. And although he had every right to draw a handsome salary, Nehemiah chose to live modestly so as not to oppress the people (Neh. 5:14–19).

Another example of Nehemiah's less-is-more lifestyle is his care for the poor and powerless. As soon as he became aware of abuse occurring among the laborers, he stopped the project midstream and put an end to the oppression. He made certain the workers wouldn't be abused by those who had been charging interest on loans and enslaving their children as collateral (Neh. 5).

What's the bottom line? Over and over, Nehemiah placed God's priorities before his own. Like Jesus, Nehemiah was a selfless servant who was not interested in amassing possessions or acquiring status. We are called to have the same attitude.

Plumb Line Principle 2: No Compromise

As far as Nehemiah was concerned, there was no justification for disregarding God's Word. For example, the law did not permit Nehemiah, as a layman, to enter the temple. So when his enemies encouraged him to run there for cover, he wasn't about to make a cowardly turn against God's commands. Even with his life at stake, Nehemiah didn't take shortcuts or transgress against the statutes in God's Word (Neh. 6:11).

Nehemiah was also committed to keeping God's regulations sacred. He never neglected the importance of worship (Neh. 12:40–43), disregarded the sanctity of the Sabbath (Neh. 13:19–22), or shrugged off his duties in God's house (Neh. 10:28–39).

In spite of everything he faced, Nehemiah didn't compromise his integrity because he revered God and highly regarded His history with mankind. The entire ninth chapter of Nehemiah includes a record of God's miracles, judgments, and deliverance of the Jews from Egyptian rule. Nehemiah knew how important it was to remember God's faithfulness in the past as well as His promises for the future.

Whether he was dealing with peasants or kings, Nehemiah consistently led a life of no compromise. He had asked King Artaxerxes for permission to leave his service as the king's cupbearer in order to rally the Jewish people to restore the city. But when the project was complete, Nehemiah left Jerusalem and humbly returned to the king's court, just as he promised (Neh. 13:6). Nehemiah was a man of his word, something that is quite rare today. God longs for His people to "become blameless and pure, children of God without fault in a warped and crooked generation" (Phil. 2:15).

Plumb Line Principle 3: No Confidence in the Flesh

Nehemiah didn't rely on his own strength to overcome his enemies. He consistently looked to God to be his strength and confidence. Despite repeated assaults, ridicule, scorn, and threats, he never conceded to the opposition. Nehemiah remained tenacious and persevered through every obstacle he encountered. When his enemies threatened to stop his forward progress, Nehemiah refused to give ear to their accusations. During the reconstruction, he didn't retaliate against his opponents but relied on God to settle every dispute and fight each battle on his behalf. Nehemiah wasn't concerned about how weak he appeared to those around him, and he wasn't too proud to ask for help. He was secure in his identity as God's very own (Neh. 4:19–20; 6:16).

In a tangible way, Nehemiah's leadership was characterized by his willingness to follow. Although he was a skillful administrator, Nehemiah didn't feel a need to call the shots all the time. Like the apostle Paul, Nehemiah knew that in his weakness, God's power would be made manifest.

Nehemiah never sought the accolades of others. His greatest concern was to be remembered as a man of God. If a record was to be kept of Nehemiah's good deeds, he wanted it noted in God's register, not in the annals of men (Neh. 13:14, 22, 31).

The three Plumb Line Principles we have described have powerful applications to your marriage. They are intentional choices—choices characteristic of Jesus, Nehemiah, Paul, and many others in the Bible—that must constitute the *culture* of your marriage, who you are as one flesh. Living the inverted lifestyle, refusing to compromise in any area of your life, and fully relying on God for all things must serve as the plumb line that keeps each of you focused on your vertical relationship with the Lord throughout your journey together. Choosing kingdom priorities over earthly pursuits grants you access to more intense pleasure and intimacy than you could ever conceive. And if that isn't enough, it's also an incredibly purposeful way to live the rest of your lives.

The Momentum to Turn the Tide

From Clint

Penny and I only realized the true power of these principles when we tried them out for ourselves. Both of us crashed and burned during the years following our divorce. Eventually, we each found ourselves in desperate straits, the bottom of the bottom. Living on opposite coasts of the United States at the time, we were broken and humbled before God, finally acknowledging that we'd made huge messes of our lives.

For me, the surrender came when I finally admitted I was angry at God for the way Penny and I had split up. Secretly, I blamed Him for our divorce. Upon confessing my anger and asking God for His forgiveness, I let go of all the coping devices I'd been harboring and all the things of earth on which I'd been building my life. Several weeks later, I darkened the doorway of a church, something I hadn't done in years. Then and only then did God allow Penny to come back into my life.

Her letter arrived on March 1, 2002. I was coming home from my job as a real estate agent. Grabbing a stack of letters and bills from the mailbox, I hurried up the front steps and put the key into the lock on the front door. When I looked down at the envelope on top of the pile, my heart sank down to my knees—and came back up. I stumbled inside the house, placed the envelope on my desk, and stared at it for a long time.

"God, should I open it—or not?"

It had been over a decade since I'd seen or heard from Penny. With a unique mixture of shock and awe, I eventually opened the envelope. Inside was a letter that read . . .

February 18, 2002
Dear Clint,

I have no idea if this letter will even reach you. I pray that it will. As a matter of fact, my intent to contact you has been bathed in prayer for almost a year. Now that I think I finally have your latest address, there's no excuse for me to hesitate any longer, except for my own fears as to how you might react, or that you will not respond. Honestly, I don't really expect anything in return from you, unless you feel led to do so. My hope is that I would at least know that you received this and read it.

My intent in writing this is to bring healing to my life and hopefully yours. It is not to bring you pain or open old wounds. As I've been actively seeking the Lord's will for my life over the last three years, one thing has been clear. He has shown me ways in which I clearly left my relationship with you unresolved. He has shown me that I made some serious mistakes with huge consequences. He has directed me to apologize to you and to ask your forgiveness. Let me start with the last.

I know that I would be crazy to think that a letter more than ten years after the fact would be adequate in admitting my wrongdoing. I know that it is not. Actually, I would prefer talking with you by phone or face-to-face because I believe you deserve that. However, I figured I'd start with a letter. If God allows this to move toward a conversation down the road, I'm game if you are.

I am very sorry for my part in the breakdown of our marriage and I do ask for your forgiveness. As I have grown older (and hopefully wiser), I have certainly seen more clearly the ways in which I contributed to our divorce. Again, mere words fail, but perhaps we'll have the opportunity to try and get it right down the road.

I also want to confess that when I was first urged to contact you, about a year ago, it was because I was dating a man and had thoughts of a future marriage, family, etc. I realized that in order to know God's will and whether or not He would even approve of a marriage, I needed to go back to heal some things from our marriage and truly seek out His answers. We are no longer dating, however, I decided that a relationship with another person is not the catalyst I should be using to make me finally contact you. I should contact you simply because it's the right thing to do, it would please the Lord, and I want my relationship with Him to be more intimate. And so, now is the right time.

I have been on my own for several years now. Solitude has drawn me to a relationship with Christ that I never thought possible. I am continually amazed by His grace and unconditional love for me, despite my many mistakes. Enclosed is a CD that might give you a better glimpse into where I am on this journey called life.

I have no doubt that you have been successful at whatever you have put your mind to. You were always very determined. I do think of you often and wonder what you are up to. It's hard to believe this much time has passed and how far apart we are. It is my hope and prayer that this letter might begin to bridge the gap between us and that God will soften your heart to consider my words.

Clint, please pray about this. Know that I will continue praying long after this letter leaves my hands and is placed into His and ultimately, yours.

Penny

From Penny

While I long to author a hundred books before I die, the most important thing I could ever write was that letter to Clint. God took the thing I hoped would bring closure to the past, and with it He burst our future wide open.

It took eleven years and some agonizing lessons in the school of hard knocks for both of us, but when the time was right, God drew in a big, deep breath and blew a whirlwind of new life into a dead marriage. We share that letter with you to illustrate and reiterate that *this* is the God of reconciliation we worship and serve.

This is our God. A God of healing and redemption.

This is *our* God! A God who plucks sinners from the misery they've made of their lives, presses their wounded souls tightly against His bosom, and makes them whole.

Like our marriage, your reconciliation is now part of the groundswell that will help turn the tide of shattered relationships and transform the face of our world from a dismal frown into one of radiant countenance. Make no mistake: every reconciled marriage delivers another deathblow deep into the gut of evil.

Dear friend, while the world wags its tail waiting for some cutting-edge politician to heal the ills that plague us, God has already given us the catalyst for true change through Jesus Christ. God is looking for people who want to be purified for a sacred purpose and who will voluntarily live a less-is-more lifestyle out of gratitude and devotion to Him. At this very moment, God is searching the earth for people who are without compromise, who place no confidence in their own flesh, and who will consciously choose to work out their faith in humble acts of profound obedience. Can you imagine what would happen in our world today if *everyone* caught on?

A Change of Season

We firmly believe God is just waiting to cut loose with an unprecedented supernatural revival on all fronts and that the threatening tide of divorce will dramatically turn back through forgiveness and reconciliation, one couple at a time. Over and over, the Bible demonstrates that God's grandeur shines forth when, in ways that are counterintuitive to the flesh, we walk in stride with the Spirit.

Until now, we have never publicly declared what we're about to disclose.

During our very first 40-Day Marriage Mission Trip in 2006,

God spoke to us distinctly about a revival of marriages and families across our nation. It all started in a living room in Ypsilanti, Michigan.

Just prior to our leaving on the mission, our ministry partners, Eric and Jennifer Garcia (founders of the Association of Marriage and Family Ministries), had asked us to pray for one month over the following verse: "If my people, who are called by my name, will humble themselves and pray and seek my face and turn from their wicked ways, then I will hear from heaven, and I will forgive their sin and will heal their land" (2 Chron. 7:14).

At the end of the month, Eric and Jennifer wanted us to report what we sensed God was saying about restoring our nation through marriage and family ministries.

In Ypsilanti, we stayed at the home of our dear friends Ben and Jennifer Freudenburg, founders of the Family Friendly Partners Network. One evening, the four of us spent time talking and praying about our shared passion for marriage and family ministry. As Clint prayed aloud in Ben and Jennifer's living room, the Holy Spirit dropped something sacred into my heart: "There will be the turning of a Fifth Season—a supernatural season of the Holy Spirit's revival upon marriages and families across this nation."

Fast-forward a few years and many more mission trips. The turning of a supernatural Fifth Season is now firmly lodged in our hearts. We believe that this Fifth Season—a season absolutely impossible in the natural realm—will be ushered in by "the God who gives life to the dead and calls into being things that were not" (Rom. 4:17). The God who can turn a shameful past into a hopeful future. The God who can breathe brand-new life into a dead marriage.

Like throwing a stone into a pond of stagnant water, the decision we made to reconcile our marriage has had a ripple effect. The same can be said for all the other couples you've met through the pages of this book. And now, the decision you've made to restore *your* marriage creates yet another surge in this holy momentum to usher the Fifth Season into greater manifestation. Having said that, whenever you're tempted to throw in the towel—and you will be tempted—remember the *eternal* significance of saving your marriage and unequivocally refuse to give up or give in.

In the introduction of this book we posed the question, *What if?* Now, at the conclusion of this final chapter, we ask it again.

What if together, as husband and wife, you decided to voluntarily live the less-is-more lifestyle? What if you made a commitment to take no shortcuts and make no compromises when it comes to restoring your marriage and family? And what if you put no confidence in the flesh but instead fixed all your hope in the power of the Holy Spirit?

Of all the qualities we've grown to love about Nehemiah, perhaps what endears him to our hearts the most is this: he never left well enough alone.

Please don't leave well enough alone—not in your marriage, your family, or your relationship with God.

Our prayer for you is this: that as you turn the last page of this book, you now possess a more insatiable hunger for God than when you opened it at the beginning.

> Burst into songs of joy together,
>   you ruins of Jerusalem,
> for the LORD has comforted his people,
>   he has redeemed Jerusalem.
> The LORD will lay bare his holy arm
>   in the sight of all the nations,
> and all the ends of the earth will see
>   the salvation of our God.
>   (Isa. 52:9–10)

God Is Just Getting Started · *3:44 minutes*

Prayer to Travel into New Territories

Gracious God, we worship You. Only You can make us whole and complete. We want more of You. Increase our appetite for Your Word. Place a greater desire for Your truth in our hearts. We give You full access to our hearts, our marriage, and our family.

Teach us how to live a less-is-more lifestyle. Holy Spirit, convict our hearts when we're tempted to compromise or take shortcuts. We confess our weaknesses and draw upon Your strength now as we continue this journey called marriage. We know that our relationship will never be fully restored until we get to heaven, but teach us how to live as one flesh in every area of our lives. May You allow us to boldly step forward into new territories of intimacy and faith with You all the days of our lives together. In Jesus' name we pray. Amen.

For a Marriage on the Mend

Making Connections

Together, spend some time in God's Word and locate at least two other Bible characters who exhibit the Plumb Line Principles discussed in this chapter. Then trace the favorable fallout from their countercultural decisions and the impact of those decisions on human history.

In addition, lay out the blank section of your marriage timeline and spend some moments together asking God to have His way with what is to come. Offer God the future of your marriage and give

Marriage on the Mend

Him permission to begin writing a whole new chapter in your lives—
one that is deeply rooted in Jesus Christ.

Questions to Consider

1. In your own words, explain the truth in the following statement from this chapter: "The wall around Jerusalem was a
   symbol of the nation itself."
2. Which of the three Plumb Line Principles spoke to your heart
   the most: (1) the less-is-more lifestyle, (2) living a life of no
   compromise, or (3) placing no confidence in the flesh? Explain
   your answer.
3. As you continue to deepen and move forward in your marriage, which tools from this book do you need to keep handy
   at all times?
4. How can you apply "Don't leave well enough alone" to your
   marriage right now?

Notes

1. "New Marriage and Divorce Statistics Released," March 31, 2008, The Barna Group, Ltd., https://www.barna.org/barna -update/article/15-familykids/42-new-marriage-and-divorce -statistics-released.

2. For information about PAIRS (Practical Application of Intimate Relationship Skills), visit http://www.pairs.com.

3. K. Kris Hirst, "Why Do Conquering Civilizations Rebuild in the Same Place?" About.com, accessed November 3, 2014, http:// archaeology.about.com/od/questionoftheweek/qt/buried _sites2.htm.

4. Gerri Begay, "Nowhere to Turn but Up," *Indian Life* (July– August 1990), 6–9. Used by permission.

5. Sylvia Gunter, *Prayer Essentials for Living in His Presence*, vol. 1 (Birmingham: The Father's Business, 2000), 153.

6. J. Vernon McGee, "The Gospel in the Gates of Jerusalem" (Pasadena, CA: Through the Bible Radio Network, nd). Download available at www.ttb.org.

7. Walter F. Adeny, *Ezra, Nehemiah, and Esther* (London: Hodder and Stoughton, 1906), 230.

8. Charles Stanley, *Living in the Power of the Holy Spirit* (Nashville: Thomas Nelson, 2005), 96–97.

9. Jeff and Cheryl Scruggs, *I Do, Again: How We Found a Second Chance at Our Marriage—and You Can Too* (Colorado Springs: WaterBrook, 2008), 109.

10. Clint and Penny Bragg, *Dance Lessons: A Weekly Devotional Guide for Couples* (Port Orange, FL: Inverse Ministries, 2004).

11. J. Vernon McGee, *Thru the Bible*, vol. 2 (Nashville: Thomas Nelson, 1982), 520–21.

About the Authors

The reconciliation of Clint and Penny Bragg's marriage after an eleven-year divorce and a three-thousand-mile, coast-to-coast separation is nothing short of a modern-day miracle. Through the work of Inverse Ministries, their nonprofit organization, the Braggs serve as marriage missionaries, sharing their testimony with audiences, teaching seminars, leading retreats, and equipping ministry leaders across the nation and abroad.

Prior to forming Inverse Ministries, Clint and Penny worked as educators in the public school system for a combined total of more than twenty years. Their story of reconciliation has been featured on local and national television and radio programs.

Originally from the San Francisco Bay area, Clint and Penny relocated in 2007 to Florida, where they now reside. Clint is an avid videographer who plans to make their testimony into a feature film. Clint also leads husbands' discipleship groups in their community. Penny is a hospice volunteer for the traumatic loss program in their area and is passionate about her mixed-media artwork and writing. In 2014, she published a grief response journal titled *For Those Who Weep*.